WHO'S TO BLAME?

WHO'S TO BLAME?

Living along society's "fault" line

Second Edition

by Dan Linssen

Copyright © 2018 by Dan Linssen. All rights reserved.
Reproduction of any part of this publication in any way requires written permission from the author.

Independently Published

ISBN – 9781717929303

Contents

Introduction _____ *1*
Our Obsession with Blame and the Resultant Costs _____ *7*
Cultural Roots of Blame _____ *15*
The Psychology of Blame _____ *25*
Situational Factors _____ *39*
Blame is Irrational (and distracts us from real causes) ___ *55*
Blame, Accountability, and Personal Responsibility _____ *69*
Reducing Blame _____ *83*
Responding to Blame _____ *103*
Afterword _____ *109*
Appendix _____ *113*
Endnotes _____ *133*

Introduction

Every society is shaped by social constructs – widely held values and beliefs that influence how people think and operate. Some societies believe in elected government designed to serve the people while other societies believe in the eminence of supreme rulers. Some societies espouse gender equality while other societies ascribe dominance to one gender. In some societies honest and frank confrontation is admired while in others such behavior is considered taboo. Often these ideas are so deeply embedded into the social fabric they seem part of the natural order of the universe. But they are just viewpoints – not necessarily reality. Sometimes these viewpoints are beneficial to the success of that culture. Sometimes they are fissures that threaten the stability of the cultural terrain.

In Western Culture one of our embedded social constructs leads us to believe that when something goes wrong, someone must be to blame in some way. Our entire legal system is built around the determination of guilt or liability for events. Our insurance industry devotes enormous resources to finding fault in loss events as a means of controlling claim payments. The concept of blame is endemic (perhaps epidemic) in Western culture. Everyday, in every aspect of our lives, we try to fix blame for things that go wrong. Bosses blame workers for sub-par organizational results. Workers blame their bosses for job dissatisfaction. Parents blame kids for actions and behaviors that don't meet their standards. Teenagers blame their parents for the restrictions on their freedoms. Adult children blame poor parenting for an assortment of personal development disorders. The poor blame the rich for the disparity in wealth. The rich blame the poor for an assortment of urban ills. Taxpayers blame government for runaway taxes, and politicians blame each other for everything!

2 Who's to Blame

Even in purely natural calamities we try to attribute the resultant suffering to someone's human failure somewhere along the line. For example, on August 29, 2005, when hurricane Katrina roared out of the Gulf of Mexico and into the Mississippi delta, the city of New Orleans was devastated by the storm surge. In its wake the storm left overwhelming human casualties, property damage, and homelessness. Only hours into the aftermath the finger-pointing began. Why hadn't the National Weather Service given more accurate forecasting? Who was at fault for failure of the dike system? Who was to blame for the slow emergency response? Blame raged among citizens; media; local, state, and national government; emergency aid organizations; plus various other culprits. So prevalent was the blame game that editorial cartoonists, late-night television comedians, and anyone with a wry sense of humor found plenty of material.

> *Yesterday President Bush made his fifth visit to the area that received the most damage from Hurricane Katrina. In other words, the White House. --Conan O'Brien*[1]

> *Even President Bush... said his administration's response to Katrina was unacceptable. Then he said "Hey, don't blame me, I was on vacation." --Jay Leno*[2]

But who really is to blame for the aftermath? Who should have better prepared for such a disaster? As a society, we could have chosen to allocate greater resources to prepare for such an event. We could have taken steps beforehand to minimize the damage caused by such a storm. Why didn't we?

If a major earthquake leveled Memphis tomorrow, or if the super-volcano under Yellowstone National Park re-erupted, or if an asteroid slammed into Cleveland, might the resultant losses have been mitigated with greater preparation? These are all potential natural events with varying degrees of probability in a specific time frame. Today it may not seem reasonable to take the kinds of actions that would dramatically curtail the attendant destruction. But in the aftermath of any such catastrophe we would likely be searching for someone to blame for the lack of preparation.

When events are dramatic and newsworthy, the search for blame takes a high profile. So when a commercial airliner attempts to take off on the wrong runway (too short) and crashes, when someone walks into a school and starts shooting, when the economy slumps and banks fail, or when a drunken driver kills innocent children, the public pressure to fix blame on someone is front and center.

But even when events are more personal or mundane we continue to search for whom to blame. So, when a business ships the wrong product to a customer, when a child gets poor grades in school, when the property tax bill is 10% higher than last year, or when someone is unhappy in his or her relationship, we still try to fix blame.

You're probably already thinking, "Well, of course we should blame those who cause bad things to happen!" Such is the power of social constructs. Our thinking seems obvious and natural. Unfortunately, fixing blame rarely solves the underlying problem. And more importantly, blame causes enormous collateral damage throughout our society. When we stop to honestly analyze our blaming behaviors we know they are not productive. Everyone intuitively understands the fallacy of "the blame game." We've developed sayings like "the buck stops here" to underscore our awareness that passing blame is not really productive. Moreover, anyone who has ever been blamed for anything feels the sense of unfairness about it. Yet, we persist in an almost obsessive connection to blame.

I'm not suggesting that a society shouldn't restrict or control damaging behaviors of its members. After all, anarchy doesn't bode well for societal sustainability. But as we'll see in Chapter 6, we can establish consequences for one's actions without judging the person's moral worth. Blame, on the other hand strikes at the core of an individual. When blaming, we impute a value judgment about the essential good or evil of that person.

After a lifetime of observing blame and its impacts (including my share of personal participation) I've developed many questions, including: Why do we do this? Is blame hard-wired into our mental circuitry, or is it a cultural phenomenon? What causes us to assign blame to specific actions in some cases but not others? Is blame necessary to an orderly society? Is it just? Are there ways to minimize the costs of blame, or to even reduce its presence in our lives?

What follows is the culmination of my search for answers. This book is not an academic dissertation built on rigorous research techniques. But the search for answers to my questions has certainly delved into varied disciplines, and has revealed insights that have changed my life. In sitting down and writing this book I was driven by the assumptions that many others: *(a)* were frustrated with the consequences of blame in their lives; *(b)* would be interested in learning more about the subject; and *(c)* aspired to reduce the impact of blame in the world around them. To that end, this book will guide you along the following path in learning about blame:

Chapter One surveys the depths of our obsession with blame and illustrates the attendant costs to our families, our society at large, and ourselves individually.

Chapters Two, Three, and Four investigate why we blame. Specifically, we examine some of the cultural, psychological, and situational underpinnings that trigger blaming behavior and support our addiction to blame.

Chapter Five explains how the entire concept of blame is built on faulty logic and fails to accomplish the intended objectives.

Chapter Six differentiates the concepts of blame, accountability, and personal responsibility and shows how we can maintain constructive accountability for socially unacceptable actions without the negative side-effects of blame.

Chapter Seven describes some interventions we can all employ to reduce our tendency to blame others.

Chapter Eight offers ideas on how to handle situations in which YOU are caught in the blame crosshairs!

Finally, I've added an appendix that deals strictly with blame in the workplace that outlines the negative impacts of blame in an organizational environment. This section includes a case study that assimilates much of the information from preceding chapters.

Those who live along nature's tectonic fault lines appreciate the dynamics of Earth's jolting idiosyncrasies. How we construct our buildings, how we adapt our lifestyle, and how we respond when such faults let loose can protect us from their ravages. Likewise, learning about the fault lines of blame ("It's your fault!") can help us improve the design of our social structures, make adaptations in our interpersonal lifestyles, and improve our response to blame-related seismic activity. Armed with the information in this book, your life along the "societal fault line" can become much more desirable.

Many of the examples throughout this book deal with blame from a leadership perspective. The realm of leadership is rife with opportunity for, and occurrences of, blame. But the lessons gleaned from these examples apply equally well to any aspect of life where one individual holds influence over another - whether through structured positions of power, interpersonal relationships, or differences of wealth, knowledge, or class distinction.

If reading this book causes you to think twice before engaging in blaming behaviors, or if it helps you redirect misguided blame focused on you, it will have been worth your time to read, and worth my time to write. Thank you for picking up the book and reading this far in the first place. When you're finished, I'd love to get your feedback. I can be reached through my website:
www.DanLinssen.com

1

Our Obsession with Blame and the Resultant Costs

If you have any doubt about blame's pervasive and obsessive presence in our social culture, try this little exercise. Go to the website of any major newspaper. In the search function type "blame." For further impact limit your search results to the current day only. See how many articles are referenced.

I was surprised to find on a single day in a major east coast publication 23 articles listed. The search for whom to blame was embedded in stories across the news spectrum including:
- The rise in college tuition
- The perception that crime is on the increase when data show otherwise
- The failure of teens to practice safe sex
- A suicide bombing in Afghanistan
- The growing nuclear threat posed by the Iranian Republican Guard
- A prominent golfer's fall from grace
- A luge death at the winter Olympics
- The declining polls of an eastern governor
- The economic collapse in Zimbabwe
- The slow reconstruction of "ground zero" in New York City

In all of these articles the reporting attempted to find fault with some individual or organization for the negative result. Minimal space was devoted to exploring the underlying structural or systemic conditions that led to these outcomes. The primary search was for whom to blame.

Evidence of our social obsession with blame also reveals itself in the litigious nature of our legal system. Billions of dollars are awarded each year to plaintiffs who blame someone found to have contributed to the plaintiff's sorrow. And not only do we need to fear being sued by someone who we inadvertently harm, but we might be sued even if we try to help someone in trouble and are unsuccessful. "Good Samaritan" suits became so common in the latter part of the 20th century that many jurisdictions eventually enacted laws to prevent a Good Samaritan from being sued (unless evidence of "negligence" is found). People have become so afraid to get involved (and risk being blamed) that some states now have "duty to assist" laws that actually require a passer-by to lend assistance to someone in trouble. To enhance the emphasis of blame in many civil suits, the courts may impose "punitive damages" that far exceed the actual loss incurred by the plaintiff. One study indicated that such punitive damages were awarded in 17 percent of all financial injury verdicts.[3]

We fare no better in the workplace where we spend a majority of our waking day. Organizational environments are highly outcome oriented. We expect positive outcomes (meeting corporate goals) and don't well tolerate negative outcomes (problems and set-backs). From the highest levels of the organization to the lowest, we attribute outcomes (positive or negative) to people. We praise those associated with positive outcomes and blame those associated with negative outcomes. So when sales fall below expectations, costs exceed budget, or even when the toilet paper roll is empty in the customer restroom, we immediately look for who is at fault. "It's a competitive world out there, and if you can't make it happen, we'll find someone who can" has probably been heard more than once in most organizations. We even develop elaborate progressive discipline processes to justify the ultimate act of organizational blame – termination of employment.

Unfortunately, sanctuary from the world of blame eludes us even in our personal relationships with others. When romantic relationships fail, we convince ourselves that fault lies with the other person. Likewise, when parent-child relations are rocky each blames the other. Interpersonal blame is so prevalent that we have built an entire profession of family and relationship counseling centered on correcting our belief that unhappiness should be blamed on those around us.

Blame is common. It's everywhere. Whether the sudden collapse of a freeway bridge, global climate change, the failure of our favorite sports team to make the playoffs, budget overruns on our assigned project, slow service at the local coffee shop, or the inability to find anything interesting on cable TV, we tend to focus on who's to blame. One could say we're blame-aholics. But is that really a big deal? Isn't blame is just a part of life, like breathing or eating? Why shouldn't we just learn to deal with it?

The reason: our obsession with blame comes with enormous costs. Some of those costs may seem small when considered individually. After one of my seminars a participant came up and relayed her story of how blame can be found in seemingly trivial family situations.

> *My husband and I had been married a short time. One day I was doing some baking that required several eggs. When I was done only two eggs remained in the carton, which I put back in the refrigerator. The next day my husband was looking for something in the refrigerator when the egg carton fell out onto the floor. Egg white and yolks seeped out onto the floor. My husband swore and stomped over to the sink for a paper towel. While wiping up the mess he opened the carton and exclaimed, "Well, no wonder!" And then he asked, "Were you the last person to put the eggs away?" I said, "Probably." He replied, "Well, look what you did! This is why the carton fell out. You left two eggs on the same end of the carton. Everyone knows you can't leave two eggs on one end because it will be unbalanced and this is what happens." He was very angry and I was hurt by the blame. It was then I realized the honeymoon was probably over. Now, twenty years later, every time I open a carton of eggs the memory of those hurt feelings returns. I'm sure my*

husband doesn't remember the incident. But for me it's been a decades-long reminder.

To me, the poignancy of this story lies in the lifetime scars deposited by what seems to be insignificant blame. Add the fact that repetitions of similar situations contribute cumulative effects, and in the end, seemingly inconsequential incidents of blame can lead to very consequential costs – like the destruction of a marriage. We obviously don't track statistics on the number of divorces each year due to blame because the specifics of blame are different in each case (although there are some very common themes). But it is safe to say that couples who resort to blaming each other instead of getting at underlying issues typically degenerate into irreconcilable conflict. What fiscal and emotional costs accrue to our society from over 14 million divorces each year? Add to that the family rifts due to blame between parents and children, and between siblings, and the costs of blame in our family structures becomes unfathomable.

The costs of blame extend beyond the family to every aspect of our society. If a surgeon leaves a sponge cloth inside the patient when closing after the surgery because he was distracted talking about the weekend ball game, he should certainly be held accountable for the consequences. But should we blame the family physician who first consulted with the patient on the need for the surgery? We do. In our healthcare system blame attributed to healthcare providers (i.e. claims of malpractice) creates real problems.

Medical liability premiums in the U.S. have increased over 2000% since 1975.[4] This has led to the emergence of what has become known as "defensive medicine" in which physicians order procedures that have little bearing on patient care, but help protect the physician from liability in case he is blamed for malpractice. Defensive medicine has substantially raised the cost of healthcare for everyone. But blame has affected access as well as cost. Over the past 30 years the increase in tort claims related to birthing and delivery has led to a marked decline in obstetricians and the closure of OB-GYN departments in hospitals across the country.

And the problem isn't limited to remote areas. In a two-year period in Philadelphia seven hospitals closed their OB departments while another three hospitals that offered OB services closed altogether.[5] In many areas pregnant women are having extreme difficulty finding access to the healthcare system.

Blame also has affected access to emergency care. One survey found that 73% of emergency departments across the country reported having inadequate on-call specialist coverage. According to the American College of Emergency Physicians President Frederick Blum, "Emergency medicine is in a state of emergency itself, and patients are suffering."[6] To what extent has our insistence on blaming others for our medical misfortunes resulted in today's healthcare crisis? That's difficult to quantify, but there's little doubt of the influence.

If a toy manufacturer produces a toy that explodes in a child's face due to careless design or use of hazardous materials we should clearly hold that producer accountable for making an unsafe toy. But should a bicycle manufacturer be blamed when a 10 year old child riding a perfectly good bicycle at night gets hit by a car on an unlit street? The degree of blame consumers attribute to producers for their unhappiness with goods purchased costs society through inflated product pricing and the inability to purchase socially beneficial products.

From the 1960s through the early 1990s producers of general aviation aircraft were increasingly blamed (i.e. sued) by crash victims and their survivors. Manufacturers were sued in 90 percent of crash incidents even though data shows that over 85 percent of crashes were due to pilot error. In some cases these suits related to aircraft produced 20 or 30 years earlier. Product liability costs rose to such dramatic levels that by the mid 1990s general aviation aircraft production in the U.S. had virtually disappeared. All three major companies had ceased production and thousands of jobs were eliminated. In 1994 Congress enacted legislation exempting aircraft older than 18 years from manufacturer liability, but the damage had been done. Today relatively few general aviation planes are built in the U.S. and costs are astronomical.[7]

You may not be in the market for a single-engine airplane so who cares, right? But consider some of these other product liability costs we incur. "The U.S. vaccine industry has been hard hit by the costs associated with liability for adverse reactions to its vaccines. Indeed, producers attribute much of the price of vaccines to costs of liability, which largely shift to consumers through higher prices. Ten of the thirteen companies manufacturing vaccines for the five serious childhood diseases exited the market because of rising liability costs."[8] According to an article in *Science* magazine, "At least two companies delayed research on an AIDS vaccine, while another company abandoned a promising approach altogether due to liability concerns."[9] Another issue of the same magazine reported, "Monsanto Company abandoned the planned production of a safe, biodegradable, and effective reinforcing phosphate fiber that would have been a substitute for asbestos."[10] Our habit of blaming manufacturers may even be shutting us off from innovations and products that could save our lives. Product liability risks currently deter research, development, and production of new products in the biotechnology industry within the United States. Not only will this place us at a competitive disadvantage in an emerging global industry in which the U.S. could take a leading role, but it will likely constrain the development of products that could extend life spans and improve quality of life.[11]

How much of the political gridlock in Washington and in state capitols around the country spawns from blame? Each party blames the other for downturns in the economy, for wars, for poor education, for poverty, or for any other social ill. How can we expect real collaboration on solutions to these issues? Except in rare moments of national unity, usually following a major crisis, blame is an endemic feature of our democracy. Since the emergence of a dual party system in the late 18th century, politicians have learned that only by blaming the other party can they hope to remain in power through re-election. We enjoy tremendous freedoms generated by our constitution. However, as long as voters rely on the soundbites of political discourse and campaign rhetoric to shape their views (instead of becoming fully engaged in learning about the issues), then politicians will benefit from blaming each other, and we will incur the costs of ineffective, politically expedient solutions to our pressing social concerns.

Put simply, the long-term, negative consequences of blame far outweigh the limited benefit we may receive from indulging in blame. Blame pushes people into emotional oblivion, tears families apart, terminates promising careers, cripples organizational achievement, inflates financial costs, limits our options, and fosters bureaucracies. And those are just the effects we've already incurred.

Think about this one: Blame carries the potential to terminate life on earth. The escalation cycle in all conflict centers around blame. So, as nuclear capability and other technologies of mass destruction continue to proliferate across the globe, where will the costs of blame ultimately take us? In the fall of 1962 the world came within an eye blink of a nuclear conflagration as the U.S. and Russia each blamed the other for the spread of atomic weapons. As nuclear weapons fall into the hands of rogue nations, and those nations blame Western culture for a host of ills, the decisions surrounding the use of such weapons may not be tempered by rational thinking.

Blame spreads a rather sobering list of consequences. You may think that the examples described herein are overblown or exaggerated. Yet history has shown that all of these costs link directly to blame in some way. If that is true, why do we persist in our obsession with blame? If an interplanetary space traveler came to Earth and observed our society he might be puzzled as to why we persist in such a self-destructive behavior. "Why do Earthlings do this?"

Human behavior is not always governed by rational thought. Why does an alcoholic continue to drink when he knows the devastation it causes? Why does a teenager engage in unprotected sex despite the known consequences of pregnancy or sexually transmitted diseases? Why does the investor continue to invest in a market that he knows is highly over-priced by any historical measure? Irrational behavior is abundant throughout the human experience, and blame is no exception. Yet if we recognize that a convergence of varied factors influences all human behavior we can begin to understand why we blame. Blame's cultural roots run deep in our social evolution. The psychology of blame is complex and compelling. And a range of situational factors can increase our propensity to assign blame in specific circumstances.

2

Cultural Roots of Blame

Where does blame come from? Have we always assigned blame for bad events since the dawn of humanity? Are some cultures more prone to blame than others? Has the nature of blame changed over time? What can we learn about our tendency to blame today by looking into the cultural precursors to blame? As a launch point to understanding our obsession with blame, this chapter looks at how blame has permeated our cultural roots.

Historical Roots

When I began my own exploration into what drives our propensity to blame I was curious to see how far back I could find compelling evidence of blaming behaviors. It didn't take long to discover that the origins of blame were apparent in the earliest of human written history. The term "scapegoat" is familiar to almost everyone. The word identifies someone unfairly saddled with fault for a bad event. But the origins of the term are quite interesting. Ancient Hebrew law provided for the atonement of communal sins through a periodic ritual or ceremony involving two goats. The first goat was killed as an offering or sacrifice to the Hebrew God. Next, the high priest, reciting certain incantations, transferred the sins of his tribe to the second goat. This goat was then banished out of the settlement and into the desert to be (presumably) consumed by the wilderness demon Azazel. Through this process of transference community members alleviated their own guilt for wrongdoings and moved forward cleansed. In the early 16th century, William Tynsdale first translated the ancient Hebrew bible into English. In describing the eviction of the goat from the community, he wrote that the goat was "suffered to escape."[12] Many linguists believe that this "escape goat" was the source of today's word "scapegoat."

For our purposes the significance of this Hebrew ceremony is that participants believed in the literal transfer of guilt for their wrongdoings. They shifted any moral consequences of their sins away from themselves and onto another creature. In more modern times, the scapegoating process continues to work much the same way. We shift any collective responsibility for wrongdoing onto an individual who subsequently takes the blame, and we move forward free of guilt. One need only tune in to the news media of your choice to readily observe that, while scapegoats have evolved from animals to humans, they are not an endangered species.

Fast forward from the scapegoats of biblical times to the middle ages in Europe. Prior to the advent of scientific thinking, superstitions explained most extraordinary events. For generations women known as white witches were believed to have supernatural powers – often used to help heal the sick or solve other problems. Bad events, such as generational plagues or crop failures, were generally attributed to the workings of the devil. As the church rose to widespread power and even political rule throughout Europe, witches became increasingly suspect as the cause of unexplainable events. Church hierarchy began to blame them for working in consort with the devil. By 1487 two Dominicans from Germany published a document called the Malleus Maleficarum, which gained popularity as a guideline on how to detect, interrogate, and punish witches.[13] Often poor or older females, often single or widowed with nobody to defend them, witches became an opportune scapegoat target, especially those with odd or offensive personal traits. As the notion of "black witches" gained prominence, convictions became easy as everyone began to look for evidence to support their suspicions. Communities were swept up in their search for individuals who might be potential witches. Once convicted, the witch was generally condemned to a cruel death. Burning at the stake was common in mainland Europe while hanging was more common in England.[14] The fascination with blaming witches continued for hundreds of years. As late as 1692 in Salem, Massachusetts, colonists joined in a frenzy of accusations, convictions, and punishment of people assumed to be witches. Today, our improved knowledge of science has mostly eliminated the belief in witchcraft, and we realize all those who were accused and put to death for hundreds of years were wrongly blamed for events outside their control.

Two relevant points about blame can be learned from our history with witch accusations. The first is: the power of belief can convince us of things that are impossible in reality. When we want to believe someone is guilty, we will find the evidence to justify our belief, no matter how implausible. While our knowledge of science today is better than in the 15th through 17th centuries, people of the era were not totally ignorant of how the world worked. A reasonable and completely objective person of the day might have deduced that witches could not be truly to blame for the events of which they were accused. But the belief in demonic power and superstition prevailed over rational thought. Even today we can find examples of blame in our workplace or in society that have very little basis in logic, but are highly driven by a desire to believe in the guilt of the accused.

The second point is: collective delusional thinking can sweep us into an hysteria of mass behavior that would be considered monstrous if done in isolation. Alleged witches were falsely blamed, tortured, and killed not only by local community fervor, but by social institutions as dominant and respected as the Catholic and Anglican churches. Unfortunately our progression to "modern times" has not diminished our tendency to believe in the demonic nature of those whom we find disagreeable, nor in our ability for collective cruelty. One need look no further than the nationalism of 1940's Nazi Germany to see evidence of both.

Metaphorical witch hunts remain with us in responding to workplace problems, social issues, and sometimes even natural disasters - as was the case with the hunt for blame after hurricane Katrina. And feeding frenzies of collective blame can still lead to mass persecution as evidenced in the Bosnian War, Israeli-Palestinian conflict, and modern Jihad.

Another early cultural example of the transference of evil takes us to a funeral wake in Medieval England. In order for the deceased to gain expedited passage to a favorable afterlife, he must first be cleansed of his sins. Enter another transfer-of-evil ritual. In this case, a plate of salt was placed on the breast of the deceased, and upon the salt was placed a slice of bread. The bread was believed to absorb the guilt and sins of the deceased. Sometimes the process was aided by religious incantations. Once the sins were transferred to the bread, a low-life mercenary (known as a "sin-eater") was hired to eat the bread, thus taking on the sins and carrying them away. The deceased was now free of guilt and ready to move on to a better place.[15] In contrast to the scapegoat, the sin-eater took on the guilt voluntarily in exchange for some meager compensation.

Modern-day parallels to sin eating are not as common as witch hunts or scapegoating. But the practice of assuming blame in exchange for compensation may be analogous to plea-bargaining in criminal law in which one agrees to plead guilty for a minor offense, with the compensation being protection from more rigorous prosecution. A variation on sin-eating may also happen in the workplace when one individual is expected to "take one for the team." It may also happen in those situations where an overly protective parent takes the blame for an act of their child in order to spare the child from consequences.

If we continue forward in time to the reign of nobility in Europe, we find yet another example of the transference of evil. By law, transgressions of the day had to be met with "appropriate" punishment. (Flogging with a willow branch was a favorite of the day.) However, punishment was transferable if you had the means or authority. Consequently, instead of being subjected to such base and demeaning treatment, royal youth typically enjoyed the luxury of a stand-in whenever they committed a punishable offense. A "whipping boy" (usually a poor young wretch) bore the scourge for the guilt of the royal misbehavior.[16]

A significant observation of the whipping boy example is that transference was available to those with abundant means or authority. Today we still see similar examples wherein those with vast wealth or positional power are able to avoid blame that would be inflicted on someone of average means. CEOs of large corporations often remain blame-free (and are even awarded extravagant bonuses) despite the financial ruin of their organizations. Likewise "executive privilege," whether explicit or implicit, is often enjoyed by top political leaders.

Historical examples of the transference of evil are not as easily found in all cultures. For example, early Hindu societies seemed to recognize that the assignment of blame to others was in some way self-delusional. An old Hindu proverb roughly states, "He who cannot dance puts the blame on the floor."[17] Moreover, the concept of Karma, one of nine fundamental beliefs of Hinduism, can be explained as the law of cause and effect by which each individual creates his own destiny through his thoughts, words, and deeds.[18] Blaming others is not consistent with this belief and therefore is not as common. Does that mean that Hindu societies are immune to blame? Not at all. Blame and corruption were common in pre-Gandhi colonial India. And today's Hindu societies are somewhat more secular, so the presence of blame is higher. For instance, despite Buddhism being the official state religion, Myanmar (formerly Burma) is racked by conflict among segments of the population and governmental factions. Each blames the other for the conflict.[19] Anecdotal evidence does seem to suggest, however, that blame may be less severe in some cultures than others.

Cultural Characteristics and Blame

Research has also found some cultural differences related to our propensity to blame. Fundamental attribution error, (see next chapter) which explains behaviors more on personality than situational factors, has been found more commonly in individualistic (i.e. western) cultures than in collectivistic (i.e. eastern) cultures.[20] These studies suggest that eastern cultures tend to attribute behavior to situational variables while western cultures tend to ascribe behaviors to individual characteristics. Consequently, blaming actions such as scapegoating would likely be more prevalent in western cultures.

Some even suggest that differences in blaming behaviors can be observed among various western cultures.

> *While criticism is freely given in France, when it is needed, finding fault with someone is another matter. You do something wrong out of ignorance, you are corrected, like a child. Blaming someone for something already done, like a traffic accident, is taboo. Never mind who was at fault. The important topic should be how to resolve the situation.*[21]

> *The term faute (fault) is very grave in the French mindset. 'Worse than a crime, it's a blunder!' were the famous words of diplomat Charles de Talleyrand (1754-1838). This thinking is one reason the French are loathe to admit being at fault for even the smallest mistakes, even in private.*[22]

While there does not appear to be any culture (on this planet) that is entirely blame-free, there do seem to be some cultural belief systems that support our tendency to blame.

Divinity

The first such belief system is *a divine notion of right and wrong*. In cultures in which the code of right and wrong emerges from interpretation of divine rule, life is viewed as a constant struggle between good and evil. The social belief system dictates that deities compete with satanic forces for the decision-making of individuals. Wrong-doing is often perceived as "giving in to temptation." Accordingly, when violations of the social code occur, the individual becomes blame-worthy for his lack of willpower to resist evil. Conversely, in cultures characterized by a more existential sense of right and wrong, the notion of wrong-doing becomes less connected to moral failure and more a matter of pragmatic consequence. Thus, blame is found less frequently, and is less personal in nature, in those cultures.

Perhaps a corollary of this notion involves the personal degree of guilt associated with some religious cultures. The abundant sense of guilt borne by people of Jewish or early Christian faiths is often good subject matter for comedians. For example:

A Jewish mother gave her son two neckties on Hanukkah. A week later when she came over to visit, the young man hurried into his bedroom, ripped off the tie he was wearing, put on one of the ties his mother had brought him, and hurried back. "Look, Mama! Isn't it gorgeous?" To which Mama replied, "What's the matter? You don't like the other one?"[23]

Catholics may prefer to own a t-shirt imprinted with, "Our Lady of Perpetual Guilt Alumnus."[24] People raised in these faiths generally relate good-heartedly to the humorous assertions and consequential reactions attributed to their guilt-heavy childhood indoctrinations. But the over-riding belief in some religious cultures that one is guilty for the disappointment of others does set the stage for easy blame attribution.

In discussing this point of divinity, guilt, and blame, someone once brought to my attention that Judeo-Christian tradition is also known for its forgiveness. That is certainly true. Most of us have been taught that "to err is human, to forgive divine." But, forgiveness might have evolved as a compensatory function to offset the initial blame. You see, I'm not sure you can forgive someone without believing that person was at fault to begin with.

Authoritarianism

The second belief system that predisposes certain cultures to blame is *the management of behavior through reward and punishment*. Primitive hunter-gatherer and agrarian societies often existed without highly structured hierarchical institutions to manage and control behavior. The greater the degree of personal independence, and the less interdependence on one another for survival, the less likely one is to blame another for wrong-doing. As societies grow in size and complexity, and as they evolve into specialization of labor, they develop extreme interdependence. To manage these interdependencies, authoritarian power structures emerge that construct a code of social norms, and assume the supervision of behavior to comply with those norms. Behaviors that support the authoritarian code are rewarded, while behaviors that oppose the code are met with punishment. That authority might be vested in the rule of government, religion, or other institutions. Wherever it resides, authoritarianism generally presumes to know Truth, with a capital "T", and has limited tolerance for disagreement with its moral and philosophical certainty. In such an authoritarian framework blame becomes a common way of dealing with non-compliance. Eventually, the society comes to believe that blame, and the threat of punishment, are required to maintain social order.

Transference of evil
The third belief system that encourages blame is *the transferability in the ownership of evil*. We may think that the literal transfer of evil was a concept only held centuries ago by societies influenced by superstitions and myth. Yet, throughout its existence, Christianity has taught the concept of imputation: that when Adam and Eve disobeyed God by eating the fruit of the tree of knowledge of good and evil, their sin was imputed or assigned to all humanity for all time. In other words, the children of Adam and Eve, their children, and successive generations would all equally bear the sins of their original parents. Thus, imputation is the in-bound transference of evil to a person at birth. In the same way, early Christian religions (Catholic, Lutheran, Eastern Orthodox, Anglican) practice the tradition of absolution, whereby individuals, after confessing their sins, are freed of those sins through the absolution process. Thus, absolution implies the out-bound transference of evil from a person. Given our continuing belief in these forms of literal transfer of evil, we can see how we become susceptible to belief in the transference of guilt from one, or many, to a person who is being blamed. And once that transfer has occurred, we validate our belief in that person's guilt through reinforcing thoughts, conversations, and actions.

All three of these belief systems exist in Western culture. So we should not be surprised that blame is commonplace around us.

Please note that the discussion of these cultural belief systems is not a judgment on their validity, or an implication that they provide no value to our social framework. The focus here is simply on their connection in setting the stage for blame.

The examples of cultural links to blame described in this chapter are far from exhaustive. Rather, they are illustrated here simply to demonstrate that the roots of blame run deep in humanity. If we hope to truly understand blame, we must appreciate and accept how we've woven blame into our culture throughout the ages. Blame is not something that has emerged with our modern technologies, our increasing population density, or our fast-paced lifestyles. It is as old as human history. And, if blame is found throughout human existence, then it must be deeply embedded in our psyche as well. In the next chapter we will examine what role human psychology plays in our patterns of blame.

3

The Psychology of Blame

Recognizing that blame has existed for millennia, and may vary to some degree by cultural norms, is intriguing. But we must also consider the psychology of blame if we hope to truly understand blame. What pushes us to blame others for bad events? Is blame a learned behavior? Is it a tool that we learn to use because of influences in our environment? Do blamers exhibit a particular psychological profile? Can we determine who is likely to be a blamer and who is not? Does something inside us all trigger blame? Is it a deep-rooted part of the human psyche that attempts to fill some inner need? Could blame even be a pathological problem deriving from brain dysfunction? This chapter presents a sampling of the varied psychological underpinnings to blame. The content here is not intended to be an academic treatise on the subject, but rather reflection on some basic concepts to help all of us better understand why we tend to blame.

Attribution Theory

Social psychologists use the term "attribution" to describe an inference one makes about the causes of events or behavior. These attributions are generally classified as either dispositional (related to an individual's personal traits, motives, or feelings) or situational (related to the circumstances surrounding an event).[25] So, for example, if I see you taking candy from a baby I might make a dispositional attribution that you are a mean-spirited, baby-hating, ne'er-do-well. I might also make a situational attribution and assume that the baby was choking on the candy and that you were merely responding as any reasonable person would.

For the past 50 years researchers have repeatedly found that people (particularly in Western cultures) have a common tendency to more heavily attribute the behavior of others to dispositional factors than to situational factors.[26] For some reason we like to assume that events are due to someone's personal influences over an outcome rather than circumstantial variables affecting that outcome. This tendency to over-rate personal factors is called "fundamental attribution error." While the existence of fundamental attribution error is well-documented, the reasons for this bias are still poorly understood.

In most cases, blame is a manifestation of fundamental attribution error. When something goes wrong, we seek to assign meaning to the event. In that process we have a tendency to look for dispositional attributions that could explain why the event occurred.

"Fred is late for work again. The guy is totally irresponsible."

"Henry forgot our anniversary. It's pretty clear he doesn't care about my feelings."

"Congressman Smith voted for the bill. He must have gotten some kind of personal deal."

Attribution theory documents that we like to attribute behavior to personal motives, so it helps us better understand the existence of blame as a social phenomenon. But, it does not fully explain why we blame. So, in our search for reasons let's look at a few other theories of psychology.

The Inner Psyche

A favorite target of psychoanalysis, which has its roots in early Freudian psychology, has been individual assumption of guilt for negative events caused by someone else. Through psychoanalysis some people find that they have internalized bad events, instead of attributing fault to those truly responsible. In these circumstances, a controlled sort of blame is intended to restore an individual's mental health. The sense of emotional release in re-assigning blame to someone else can be very powerful.

In the 1980s and 1990s the search for whom to blame through psychoanalysis spilled into popular culture. An epidemic of practitioners (many without appropriate credentials in psychology) began to suggest that individuals try to recall incidents of childhood sexual abuse as an explanation for a host of mental illness symptoms experienced in adulthood. By facing these childhood incidents (whether real or imagined), and fixing blame where it supposedly belonged, these patients would then be free to leave the past behind and move on with a productive life. In the highly popular (and highly criticized) book *The Courage to Heal* authors Bass and Davis suggested that if your adult life displays a certain set of symptoms, and if you think you might have been sexually abused as a child, then you were.[27] While many patients who explored this line of treatment found a degree of satisfaction (assigning blame does feel good) many families were unjustly torn apart by the accusations.

Viewing blame from the perspective of psychoanalysis reveals a complex psychological phenomenon. Avoiding the pain of our own accountability is largely a subconscious process, so we do not usually recognize our behavior as blame. Instead we feel like we're holding someone else properly accountable for the bad thing that happened. Blaming behaviors that originate so deep within the individual psyche are difficult to acknowledge at the purely conscious level.

The Behaviorist View

Exposure to blame arrives at an early age, so the prospect that blame is a learned behavior seems intuitive. Most students of introductory psychology are familiar with B.F. Skinner's theories of operant conditioning which suggest that behavior results from an individual's response to events that occur in their environment.[28] If a person's response produces a positive outcome, and if that positive outcome (reward) is reinforced each time the person responds the same way, then a behavior is learned.

Suppose seven year-old Johnny came in from playing outside and didn't fully close the door behind him. A few minutes later Ol' Yeller, the family's freedom-loving Labrador, noticed the opportunity and bounded outside to terrorize the neighborhood. When called to task by his mom for this jail-break, Johnny pleaded that he had closed the door tightly, and that it must have been his four year-old brother Jimmy who left the door unlatched. If Mom buys this argument Johnny successfully transfers the violation to little Jimmy – a positive outcome for Johnny. Assuming he again uses the same tactic when the toilet seat is left up and Ol' Yeller turns the bathroom into a soggy mess, and assuming his positive outcome is once again reinforced, Johnny begins to learn that blame can be a useful tool in avoiding the unpleasant side effects of accountability. But where did Johnny pick up the idea to transfer blame in the first place?

The behavioral psychologist Albert Bandura conducted a number of experiments to show that a repetitive stimulus-response type of consequence was not necessary for learned behaviors to take place. Instead, Bandura demonstrated that we can learn behaviors simply through observing someone else's activity.[29] One of Bandura's more famous series of experiments involved showing pre-school age children a video of other children mercilessly pummeling an inflatable BoBo doll. These children were then brought to a play area and provided access to a BoBo doll of their own. They immediately took to their own inflatable punching toy with the same vigor and aggression. According to Bandura this more cognitive approach to learned behavior involves four steps:

- Attention – noticing something in the environment
- Retention – remembering what was noticed
- Reproduction – duplicating the action that was noticed
- Motivation – the environment delivers a positive outcome

Tying this learning process back to blame, suppose that when Johnny was only five (and Ol' Yeller was just a puppy) they were playing together on the family room floor. Suddenly "young" Yeller stopped playing, and squatted on the carpet with a determined look on his face. Johnny knew what this meant as he had seen it happen before. So he scooped up Yeller and bolted for the door. Unfortunately, in his hurry, he happened to knock Aunt Edna's heirloom lamp off its table, crashing to the floor where, like Humpty-Dumpty, it lay in more pieces than could be put back together again. Yeller never made it to the door, so the mess was compounded. Mom, who (unbeknownst to Johnny) was not having a good day to begin with, roared upon the scene with a fury. Johnny received a blameful tongue-lashing for playing so carelessly and for allowing Yeller to do his duty on the carpet. After a swift spanking, Johnny was sent to his room and television privileges were revoked until dinner time.

Through Bandura's description of first-hand observational learning, Johnny probably picked up three well-remembered lessons about blame that day:
- Blame is effective at inflicting pain upon the receiver.
- Blame isn't always justified.
- Blame is a tool of authority in responding to a bad situation.

All three of these lessons would likely be filed away for later use.

Locus of Control

Perhaps those with a certain psychological profile exhibit a greater propensity towards blame. If so, a possible place to begin looking is within a concept called "locus of control." Largely attributed to Julian Rotter's work in the 1960's locus of control essentially means that some people view their experiences as a result of forces outside of themselves (an external locus of control) while other people believe that they control their own destiny (an internal locus of control).[30] For example, one traveler (external locus of control) who just missed his airline flight might believe that the cause was due to the traffic jam on the way to the airport, the long lines at security, and the date being Friday the 13th. At the same time the other traveler (internal locus of control) who missed the same flight is saying to herself, "I knew I shouldn't have hit the 'snooze' button on my alarm for the third time."

Rotter proposed that we all lie somewhere along a continuum. Those at the "external" extreme believe that events occurring in their lives are largely beyond their influence, and that fate, or destiny, or the gods, or luck determine what happens. Those at the "internal" extreme believe that events are primarily due to the actions they've taken to shape those outcomes. Most people do not lie at the extremes, but probably do have a tendency to lean one way or the other. (There are several fun and informative online surveys you can take - some free, some not - to determine your own locus of control.)[31]

What might this have to do with blame? In general, those with an internal locus of control are less likely to blame others when things go wrong. They believe that their own actions have contributed to or shaped the current problem in some way and are quick to begin looking for how to change the situation instead of blaming. Those with an external locus of control are more likely to blame forces outside of themselves for the problem. They believe that some person or event is responsible for the problem and that they are merely the victims of circumstance.

Bert and Ernie were each recently issued speeding tickets while driving along a 4-lane boulevard in a commercial district. The speed zone was 25 miles-per-hour. They were both ticketed for going 40. Both were frustrated. However, Bert (an external) blamed the municipality for setting such a low speed limit on such a wide-open street; he blamed the officer for not considering the lack of other traffic at the time; he blamed the person whom he was driving to meet (if not for the appointment he wouldn't have been there); and he blamed all the other speeding drivers who didn't get ticketed. Ernie (an internal) said to himself, "Dang, I finally got caught."

Dispositional Optimism

The optimist sees the doughnut, the pessimist sees the hole. – Anonymous

Another profiling characteristic we can examine is degree of optimism or pessimism. We intuitively understand that some people see the world as a cup half-empty, while others view it as a cup half-full. Thomas Edison is often recognized for his abundant optimism. At one point, when asked about his thousands of failed attempts to develop an electric light bulb, Edison is allegedly quoted as having said, "I've not failed once, I've just found 10,000 ways that won't work." But even when Edison's most ambitious project – an iron ore processing company in Pennsylvania – collapsed after an enormous investment in capital, effort, and 10 years of time, the inventor refused to blame others. When a co-investor complained to Edison that they had lost millions, Edison supposedly replied, "Yes, but we had a hell of a good time spending it."[32] Can optimism be measured? And if so, to what extent does optimism impact blaming behaviors?

Throughout the 1980s Scheier and Carver developed constructs to measure an individual's level of "dispositional optimism" as they called it.[33] Dispositional optimism is a general expectation that good things will happen. People with high dispositional optimism tend to stay focused on reducing the gap between where they are now and where their goals would place them. People with low dispositional optimism are more easily diverted from goal-directed behavior to more fatalistic behaviors. Subsequent studies of students and athletes by Martin Seligman supported this notion.[34] Seligman studied students who received lower grades or a slower time in athletic events and found that optimists rose to the occasion, increased goal-oriented behaviors, and did better the second time around. Pessimists, on the other hand, conceded defeat, abandoned goal-oriented behaviors, and did worse the second time around. Based on these findings one might hypothesize that individuals with high levels of dispositional optimism would be less likely to blame others for their circumstances, while those with low optimism would be more likely to assign blame for their circumstances.

Cognitive Dissonance

In the 1950s the psychologist Leon Festinger blazed a new trail into a frontier of study that eventually became known as cognitive dissonance.[35] Cognitive dissonance is the unsettled internal feeling that comes from trying to reconcile two contradictory beliefs or ideas. It has been demonstrated in numerous research projects throughout the years and shows up in many facets of our daily lives. An oft-cited illustration of the phenomena is Aesop's fable of *The Fox and the Grapes*. A hungry fox eyes a cluster of tasty-looking grapes and, despite multiple attempts to reach them, is left frustrated – he wants the grapes, but he realizes he can't get to them. In the end he resolves this conflict by deciding that the grapes are probably sour and he doesn't really want them after all.

One of the more powerful causes of dissonance arises when a belief or idea conflicts with a core element of self-concept. For example, you know you are a smart, talented individual. Yet, something in your life is going wrong. That's dissonance. How can this lead to blame? Suppose you are a mid-level manager who recently hired a project leader for your department. You have selected an accomplished, experienced candidate even though your division manager strongly preferred a promising young college graduate. For the first couple of months you look like a genius because your candidate apparently does all the right things – preparing a project plan, building rapport with related departments, and so on. But then the project runs into major trouble and grinds to a halt. You are now faced with conflicting beliefs (cognitive dissonance). You feel you made a brilliant hiring choice, but you're also painfully aware the project is currently dead in the water. How can that be? What will you do? Pulling your new hire from the project now will shine the spotlight on your apparent hiring mistake, and the delays involved in getting someone new on board and up to speed will push the project past its absolute deadline.

To the extent that you are human, you will feel a tremendous temptation to reduce dissonance by blaming someone else for the mess. After all, Finance has held up funding for key equipment, you haven't gotten the test results back from R&D that you were promised, Marketing never really gave you good requirements from the customer, and Building Maintenance still hasn't fixed the air conditioning in your new project leader's office so his work efficiency has been impaired. To the extent that you can build a compelling blame case, you will reduce the dissonance you feel about the situation. If the stalled project can be attributed to someone else, then you likely made the right hiring choice after all. Unfortunately, while blame may have reduced your dissonance, it hasn't solved the underlying problem.

Or, consider the young couple who meet on spring break in Cancun. Over the week they have the time of their lives and fall madly in love. Fate must have brought two such soul-mates together, because no two people could be more perfect for each other. Upon returning home to college they excitedly decide to lease an apartment and move in together, and they soon announce their engagement to all their family and friends. However, over the next few months she begins to realize how annoying his friends are (and they are over at the apartment all the time). At the same time, he cannot believe how demanding she is of his time. He can't seem to have a life of his own. Neither is sure they really love each other anymore. Ending the relationship would be painful enough, but it would also be embarrassing since they made such a big deal of things to everyone. Moreover, the logistics would be difficult since they've signed a one-year lease. Undoubtedly both individuals are struggling with tremendous dissonance. On the one hand each believes they had picked the perfect partner. Things were wonderful on spring break. On the other hand, they are currently dismayed by the reality of living with each other. Once again, the temptation will be to resolve the dissonance by blame. He contends that she deceptively portrayed herself as easy-going. She accuses him of becoming a couch-potato, video-gaming junkie. Unfortunately once again, while the blame may reduce the dissonance, it certainly won't solve the underlying problem.

Or, suppose you vote for a political candidate who has swept you off your feet. This fresh face holds promise of changing the entire political character of Washington DC. However, three years later the economy still struggles, military conflicts still rage around the globe, Social Security continues to slide towards bankruptcy, and shady deals continue to plague the culture of the capitol. You believed the promises of your candidate. But he hasn't been able to deliver on those promises. The dissonance is almost palpable. Some might choose to reduce their dissonance through cynicism: "All politicians are deceitful and incapable." But you choose to rely on blame: "The obstruction of the other political party has prevented my candidate from achieving success." Once again, dissonance is reduced to tolerable levels, but underlying problems remain.

Self-justification

Once we take the step of reducing cognitive dissonance by assigning blame we have a tendency to continue building and fortifying our case. We begin to see only the evidence that supports our blame, and we ignore or discount evidence to the contrary. In Thomas Kuhn's 1962 book, *The Structure of Scientific Revolutions*, the author demonstrated that once scientists formulated a hypothesis, their search for supporting evidence was almost always biased.[36] Kuhn suggested that the adoption of a paradigm or master view of how the natural world worked caused the scientist to see very clearly data that concurred with this master view. But the scientist had a hard time seeing data that conflicted with this view. Subconsciously, the scientist would continue moving down a path of research that justified his view. Later, in the 1980s, Joel Barker extrapolated this concept of paradigm shift to the corporate world in his book, *Paradigms: The Business of Discovering the Future.*[37] Barker explained how paradigms shape the master view of business and individuals, causing them to continue justifying long-held beliefs while simultaneously blinding them to realities that conflict with those beliefs. The same psychological process operates once we've attributed blame to someone. We begin to justify why we are correct in that attribution, and over time we become continually more convinced of the person's culpability for the problem.

Self-justification may not be a root-cause of blaming behavior, but it definitely reassures us that blame was warranted. In the book

Mistakes Were Made (but not by me), authors Carol Tavris and Elliot Aronson offer a conceptual model of self-justification represented by a pyramid.[38] Standing at the top of the pyramid, when confronting dissonance, you have a choice of directions in which to proceed. However, once you step off the top with an initial decision, your path to the bottom deposits you at a very different place than if you had chosen to go the other direction. All the way down your side of the pyramid you will be gathering justification for why you have chosen this direction. By the time you reach the base you will be convinced you are standing at the correct place and someone on the other side of the pyramid is in the wrong place.

When we place blame in the lap of others, this self-justification process reassures us we've made the right decision. Criminal detective movies or television shows often portray the overzealous investigator who believes someone is guilty of the crime and then relentlessly seeks out evidence to justify the conviction. But in a final twist of plot someone else turns out to be the real perpetrator. Unfortunately, wrongful convictions are not just good fiction story lines. The Innocence Project is a national organization dedicated to exonerating wrongfully convicted people. Through DNA testing and other comprehensive evidence gathering means The Innocence Project has successfully overturned convictions on hundreds of imprisoned individuals – people who were wrongly blamed for serious crimes. Many of these initial convictions were likely the result of the path of self-justification once the prosecuting team (investigators, attorneys, jury, judge) convinced themselves that the person was blameworthy of the crime.

A good example of how we are all influenced by self justification was the evolution of public support for America's war in Iraq. On March 17, 2003, literally hours before the commencement of military action against Iraq, ABCNEWS/*Washington Post* conducted a poll of support among the U.S. population.[39] 71 percent of Americans supported going to war (82 percent of men, 60 percent of women). Even 54 percent of Democrats supported war action. 66 percent of Americans supported abandoning a U.N. Security Council vote and going it alone. This support existed despite the fact that 62 percent felt going to war would increase the risk of terrorism to the U.S. in the short run. And the objective wasn't simply to eliminate weapons of mass destruction. Two-thirds said the U.S. should continue to try to oust Saddam Hussein even if he cooperated fully with U.N. weapons inspectors. One year later, according to a CNN/Opinion Research Corporation poll, only 48 percent supported the war. And by March of 2007 less than one-third of Americans supported the war. A full 90 percent of Democrats now opposed the war.[40]

Once it became apparent there were no weapons of mass destruction, once it became apparent the toppling of the Hussein government led to sectarian chaos and social disorder, and once it became apparent that insurgent resistance was claiming thousands of American lives, collective America either needed someone to blame or would have to confront the dissonant reality that it had messed up pretty badly. To make matters worse, having now destroyed the government and infrastructure of a sovereign country, thrown the nation into civil unrest (if not outright civil war), and opened the floodgates on terrorist intervention into Iraq, walking away at that point was not a very attractive option. Cognitive dissonance soared. Prior to action, most Americans thought we ought to give Saddam his due, but the outcome turned out very differently than we expected. So, to resolve dissonance, we transferred responsibility and placed blame. The Iraqi conflict became "Bush's War." The President (and Vice President, Secretary of Defense, and C.I.A.) were responsible. Self-justification began to support our blame. This mess wasn't the average citizen's fault. We were all hoodwinked into believing there were weapons of mass destruction. We were told Saddam Hussein was a sponsor of international terrorism. How could we know there would be sectarian conflict once the Iraqi government was destroyed? Self-justification quickly absolved the average American from any associated responsibility once we had someone to blame for the problem. And Democrats had the added bonus of a windfall political target – the Republicans were responsible. By the time the 2008 elections had rolled around most Americans had successfully absolved themselves of any responsibility for the conflict, and instead, transferred blame to those officials who led us into the conflict.

Congress would not likely have authorized the Iraq War Resolution in 2003 if there had only been limited public support. The push for war came from across America. In reality, everyone who supported military action is responsible for the result. But few today will say, "Yes, I supported the war and made a big mistake." Instead we have resolved the dissonance by attributing blame to the people in office at the time. And we've continued to justify that blame to such extent that today most people's conscience is free of any guilt associated with what history proved to be a national mistake.

While convictions of innocent people and declarations of war are dramatic examples, consider how, over time, self-justification cements blame for the scapegoat in the workplace, the parent who allegedly caused one's mental health issues, the teacher viewed as responsible for Johnny's failure in school, or the spouse perceived as the cause of one's boredom with life.

Other Possible Psychological Explanations

Blame offers considerable emotional appeal. Specifically, blame is easy. It doesn't require a lot of contemplation or mental anguish. When a problem occurs you simply find the culprit, administer punishment (a.k.a. corrective action or intervention) and get back to life as usual.

Blame is black and white. It's not burdened with nuanced shades of gray. Real problem solving gets very messy and requires root cause analysis, consideration of contributory effect, probability assessment, measuring degrees of uncertainly, and so on. Blame bypasses all that complexity with an air of clarity.

A more subconscious motivation to blame is the false sense of closure. One always feels great satisfaction when announcing "mission accomplished" (whether it really is or not). So, once we've blamed someone we feel like we've gotten something done.

Blame supports and reinforces our self-perception of righteousness. When we blame someone else we perceive ourselves on the moral high ground. In the end, justice is served and our value system preserved in the world around us.

Blame serves a self-protection function. When blaming others, we divert culpability for the problem away from ourselves. In most circumstances putting distance between us and a problem means fewer negative consequences than allowing ourselves to become implicated in the problem.

Finally, while the potential psychological underpinnings to blame are numerous, perhaps many people engage in blaming behaviors simply because they don't know any better. Given that blame has been part of human culture since early recorded history, and given that we're surrounded with blame in our daily lives, many people simply accept blame as normal behavior. Maybe blame is just what people do when they find someone close to the scene of a problem.

Perhaps if research psychologists someday determine a concrete cause for blame, they might also develop a pharmaceutical solution. "36-hour Blame-away?" In the meantime, the more we understand these various psychological contributors to blame, the better chance we have of managing its influence in our lives.

4

Situational Factors

In the previous chapter we saw how a variety of psychological triggers can give rise to blaming behaviors. But blame is also conditioned upon a number of different situational factors. Life is full of random unfairness, and the attribution of blame is no exception. Two people performing nearly identical actions and driven by comparable motivations can be subjected to varying degrees of blame depending upon circumstances well beyond their control. Even as a child you probably observed situations in which someone else got away with behavior that yielded blame and punishment to you. It may have been the playground teacher who looked the other way when Jimmy got a little too aggressive and shoved his playmate to the ground. Whereas, when you shoved Larry for calling you names, the same teacher sent you to see the principal. In adulthood the inequity of blame seems even more pronounced in the workplace, in our private lives, and especially in society at large. Why does one person get away with obvious bad deeds while another seems severely punished for lesser infractions? In this chapter we'll look into the circumstances and situations in which blame is more common than in others, and we'll consider what factors make an individual more or less susceptible to being blamed.

Being Different
Since the dawn of humanity we've been wary, suspicious, mistrustful, and sometimes even spiteful and hateful of those different from us in some identifiable way. We should not be

surprised, then, to realize that we use blame much more aggressively on "outsiders" than on those we consider part of our affiliated group. It doesn't matter if that group is based on age, race, nationality, economic status, educational level, religion, political affiliation, how we dress, the music we listen to, or even the football team we support. The difference might be by clique, as in high school (the jocks, geeks, nerds, gear-heads, etc.). The difference might be between the employees who worked for the acquired company and those who work for the acquiring company. The difference might be between those on the board who have a membership to the golf club and those who don't. In any case, if we are identifiably different from "the herd" our chances of being blamed for bad events go up substantially.

Blaming those who are different is most obvious in armed conflicts. The "enemy" is always to blame for whatever differences have ignited the conflict – no matter which side you're on. We intensify the focus on the differences between "us" and "them," ultimately demonizing all those with that same differentiating characteristic (despite the overwhelming similarities that always exist). They become "Jerries" or "Gooks" or "The Axis of Evil" in order to solidify our differences and increase the blame for the conflict. In the 1960s, Catholic nationalists in Ireland blamed Protestant unionists for discrimination while the unionists blamed the nationalists for insurrection. The consequence was guerilla warfare that flamed for 30 years. In Rawanda, in 1994, Hutu tribes blamed Tutsis of trying to enslave Hutu people. The Hutus responded with genocide, killing nearly a million Tutsis. And even in the aftermath of the Bosnian War few can accurately pinpoint what specific issues actually ignited the conflict. But the Bosnians, Serbians, and Croatians all blame each other for the conflict. On a smaller scale, rival gangs blame each other for inter-gang conflict and consequently continue a spiral of escalating violence. In all of these situations someone from outside the realm of conflict can see the tremendous similarities in the people involved. But from within the conflict, the relatively minor differentiating characteristics of each group have been elevated to the point of justifying murder or even genocide.

While these represent extreme examples of blame fueled by differentiation, the same phenomenon permeates the attribution of blame in more everyday cases. Gun control advocates and gun owners definitely view each other as the extremist, outsider party – the ones who are different. If crime rises in a large city gun control advocates will blame gun owners for the propagation of weapons that then fall into the hands of criminals. At the same time the gun owners blame gun control advocates because laws have become so restrictive that only criminals have guns and law abiding citizens are left defenseless. Instead of exploring common ground (like reducing crime) they position each other as the enemy and harden their positions of blame. Likewise, Democrats and Republicans continually portray each other as the out-of-touch outsiders – different from the rest of America. So, if the economy declines, Republicans will blame Democrats for high taxes that have stifled business investment. Meanwhile, Democrats will blame Republicans for blocking better programs that could have stimulated the economy with government assistance funds. Instead of truly exploring common ground (like improving the economy) they position each other as the enemy and harden their positions of blame.

But the most common examples of group differentiation occur at the more personal levels. Over time, subtle discriminations cast an individual as the outsider, and then, through gossip and incriminations, the person slowly becomes the scapegoat. Just as most school playgrounds contain a few unfortunate kids who get picked on because of their differences, most workplaces and many social groups have individuals who become the common target for blame.

Jack was recently hired as maintenance supervisor at a privately-held manufacturing plant (TEAM Co). Most of his peer-level associates at the company, along with the plant manager, had worked at TEAM for a long time and had developed a close social bond outside of work. Many of them belonged to the community summer softball league and also to a winter bowling league. Even the few who weren't on the leagues often attended social events with the others on weekends. Periodically some of the old-timers would invite Jack to join their social events. Jack, however, was not really interested in participating outside of work. He didn't dislike any of the others. In fact, he thought they were all nice folks and good at their jobs. He just preferred to be at home with his family and work on several of his personal hobbies like model railroading and restoring his vintage model A Ford.

Over time, as problems occurred in the plant, Jack increasingly began to take the heat for the issues. Somehow production failures always seemed to result from Jack's inability to stay on top of plant maintenance. So even though he was continually pressing to implement periodic shutdowns for routine preventive maintenance (and always denied) he was to blame when a breakdown occurred. And even though he tried to get TEAM to spend some money improving its water discharge system, he was to blame when the state issued a citation for violating discharge levels. After about two years, the plant manager placed Jack on written warning for his inability to provide the kinds of support needed by his peers to keep the plant running smoothly. According to the plant manager Jack lacked rapport with the departments he served and needed to get more "in synch" with the company's priorities. Eventually Jack took a job at a large, national industrial company and went on to enjoy a very successful career.

To what extent was Jack's blame for the problems at TEAM a result of the fact that he never became part of the group and was always viewed as an outsider? That's impossible to know for sure. But Jack's success in a subsequent corporate culture indicates that the issue wasn't his technical abilities. These kinds of situations are widespread in organizations of every type. And when someone stands out as different from the cultural norm, they frequently become the scapegoat for problems that occur.

Ironically, as a nation and a culture we identify ourselves with individualism. Yet, if that individualism separates you from some homogenous characteristic of your reference group, you may become the target for blame.

Severity of Outcome

If it's bad, heads will roll. One of the more fascinating situational variables to blame is the severity of outcome. The exact same action, decision, or behavior can result in dramatically different levels of blame purely on the random chance of the outcome. Severe outcomes engender severe blame while inconsequential outcomes generally attract little or no blame. That raises an interesting philosophical question. When we blame someone are we really blaming their behavior, or are we blaming the chance outcome?

On a summer night in June of 2008 an intoxicated woman was driving her Porsche on a major commercial street in Green Bay, WI. According to witnesses she got involved in a drag race with another car and reached speeds of 70 to 80 miles per hour. Approaching a controlled intersection she ran through a red light. Tragically, two teenage girls on the cross street with the green light pulled out into the intersection at the exact same moment as the Porsche entered the intersection. They were killed upon impact. The woman was convicted of reckless homicide, and homicide by intoxicated use of a motor vehicle, and sentenced to 80 years in prison.[41]

Few would argue that the woman deserved to be held accountable for the accident. But what if the timing of the event had been altered by just one second? The Porsche would have missed the car carrying the teenage girls and there might have been no consequential outcome at all. The woman might have continued on home with no more impact than a hangover the next morning. Or, maybe, she might have been stopped by the police and issued an Operating While Intoxicated (OWI) citation and incurred a modest fine. In either case, she might have joked about the incident with her friends the next day, with no blame. Identical behavior, motives, and decision-making occurred, but one second made the difference between no blame and an 80 year prison sentence with intense social blame. Millions of people have driven while intoxicated. Millions more have sped way too fast in their cars. Shouldn't they all receive the same degree of blame? The only difference is that luck spared them all a tragic consequence. Clearly blame can be a wicked game of chance. If you encounter a severe outcome your blame can be brutal, but if the outcome is inconsequential you will usually avoid blame.

Interestingly, sometimes the same decision that can potentially lead to a negative outcome can also lead to a positive outcome, in which case luck can determine if you will be blamed, or be viewed as a hero. In June of 1995, during the Bosnian peace-keeping mission, an American pilot, Captain Scott O'Grady, was shot down over Serbian territory. Captain O'Grady stayed alive for five days behind enemy lines using the most basic of survival tactics, like eating insects and collecting water from leaves. O'Grady was out of communication with the Allied Forces Command for those five days until he was able to climb a tall hill and make radio contact. At that point, the commanding officers had a difficult decision to make. Launching an immediate rescue, while still dark, but without supporting air cover, posed a significant risk to all the lives of the entire rescue team. Waiting for daylight and air support greatly increased the risk of capture (and execution) for O'Grady. Admiral Leighton Smith, Commander of the Bosnian Peacekeeping Forces, called the Marine Colonel, Martin Berndt, who would be responsible for the rescue.[42] Legend is told that during their conversation Adm. Smith commented to Col. Berndt, "Marty, if this doesn't go well, we'll both be selling shoes on Monday morning." While there were some dicey moments, the rescue concluded successfully. O'Grady and his rescuers were all hailed as heroes.

Whether the comment is fact or fiction, there is little doubt Admiral Smith was well aware that this decision could yield dichotomous results. If everything turned out well, and O'Grady was rescued without loss to the rescue team, then parades and photo-ops would await. On the other hand, if the rescue team encountered casualties or complete disaster, the blame would likely take a toll reaching all the way up the chain of command.

This incident illustrates one of the greatest shortcomings of blame as a response to bad events. In many cases, the decisions and actions that lead to an outcome must be made before the outcome could ever be known. Decisions made by managers in allocating organizational resources, decisions made by parents in guiding their children, and decisions made by anyone that might impact someone else are all made without certainty of outcomes. If the outcomes are good, blame will be avoided. However, if outcomes are bad, the decision-maker faces blame for a poor decision.

Perceived Knowledge or Authority

If you are perceived as someone who has significant knowledge about a situation (or should have knowledge based upon your position) you are more likely to be blamed for a bad outcome than someone who is perceived to have little or no knowledge about the situation.

Seated in front of an irate congressional panel in October of 2008, Alan Greenspan, former Chairman of the Federal Reserve, was taking stinging blame for the meltdown in the U.S. economy. For 40 years he was regarded as America's maven of economic knowledge. Now he sat humbled as "Democratic lawmakers asked him time and again whether he had been wrong, why he had been wrong, and whether he was sorry."[43] How could he, of all people, have failed to warn Congress of the growing house of cards in the financial industry and the simultaneous housing bubble? If he had properly informed Congress of the pending disaster they could have responded with appropriate regulation and saved the day. While there was plenty of blame to go around (Time Magazine identified "25 People to Blame for the Financial Crisis" – Greenspan ranked number three[44]) the former Fed Chair was viewed as blameworthy because he possessed a higher degree of "perceived knowledge" about America's economy than potentially anyone else.

In similar fashion, if you have positional authority over circumstances surrounding a negative event you are more likely to be blamed for the problem than if you had little line of authority or influence. This attachment holds true even if you had no direct knowledge of the event. In 2004 a small group of U.S. Army reservists handling guard duty at the Abu Ghraib prison in Iraq subjected prisoners to degrading and humiliating acts. Photographs of the acts became public and caused a firestorm of humanitarian response. The pointer of blame quickly moved up the chain of command from the reservists to their unit leaders, to the commander of the prison, to the commander of U.S. forces in Iraq, all the way to then Secretary of Defense, Donald Rumsfeld. A commission set up to investigate the scandal accused Rumsfeld of failing to exercise sufficiently rigorous oversight that would have prevented the abuse[45]. Given that U.S. regular and reserve forces total over 2 million people, it is highly unlikely that Rumsfeld had any knowledge of the specific actions occurring by this group of prison guards. And it is equally unlikely that any Secretary of Defense could ever implement sufficient controls to prevent all potential kinds of abusive violations by any member of the Armed Forces. Nonetheless, the political heat generated by this blame caused Rumsfeld to submit his offer of resignation to the President (who declined to accept it).

Coaches of sports teams frequently find themselves afflicted by this situational variable. Every season in baseball, football, basketball, or any team sport, a number of coaches end up on the chopping block due to a losing season. Some of these losing seasons are indeed a result of poor coaching and play-calling, in which case the termination seems to be warranted. But every year some coaches released by one team move to another organization and are suddenly reigning over high-performing teams. It is unlikely that their coaching prowess was suddenly transformed by the organizational switch. More likely, the blame received for the prior poor seasons was mainly a result of being caught at the helm of a sinking ship. And they happened to be in positions of knowledge and authority.

In government, business, education, science, sports, or any kind of organization, we believe that those in positions of high authority are blameworthy for actions within their organizations, no matter how remote or far-removed that action might be from the daily influence of the authority figure. If someone is believed to possess both perceived knowledge of the wrong-doing plus positional authority to prevent the event, then blame is even more likely. Parents frequently find themselves in this position. As parents they are commonly perceived to have knowledge of the behaviors and motivations of their children, and they are assumed to have authority over the actions of their children. The mother of the child throwing a temper tantrum in the grocery store knows well the message in the glaring eyes of other shoppers: "Why can't you control your child?" But parental blame can be much more serious.

In 1997, in Pearl, Mississippi, a 16 year-old boy stabbed his mother to death, then subsequently shot nine students at his school. The mother of one of the victims sued the boy's father. In 1998, in Jonesboro, Arkansas, two boys, aged 11 and 13, staged a false fire alarm, then opened fire on the exiting crowd. The parents were sued by families of those killed. And even more infamously, 5 weeks after the shootings at a Columbine, Colorado high school by two teenage boys, the parents of the shooters faced a lawsuit seeking $250 million contending that the parents should have prevented the rampage.[46] In a CBS News poll 40% of Americans blamed the incident on lack of attention by the parents[47] A subsequent poll conducted by Luntz Research found that 65% of Americans agree that, "the parents of children who commit gun-related crimes should be held accountable by being prosecuted for negligence."[48] This can be a disheartening prospect for any parent who thinks they understand their children, and who can only hope to exert a directional influence on their children's lives.

Empathy with Circumstances

Familiarity with a set of circumstances, or at least relating to the situation, can increase empathy for the person involved in the negative event. And, as empathy increases, the degree of blameworthiness decreases. If you live in a part of the country subject to cold and snowy winters, and you read about someone who inadvertently skidded off the road in a blizzard (minor damage, no injuries) you probably are inclined to go easy on the blame. You may have been in the same situation yourself, or at least come close. But if you read about an airline pilot who skids off the runway in the same blizzard (minor damage, no injuries) your attributions of blame are likely to increase. The thought of being in a commercial jet as it slides off a runway is rather terrifying to many. We would expect that such an event should not happen and would begin to search for whom to blame.

To what degree do empathy and familiarity with circumstances influence blame when the event at hand involves something horribly tragic, such as the inadvertent death of another? Consider your own tendency to assign blame in each of the following tragedies which are all based on real incidents:

Scenario One:
A good-natured, well-liked, local politician and his wife were babysitting their 2 year-old granddaughter while her parents were at work. Mid-morning, the grandfather had to leave for a meeting. As he backed his car out of the driveway he inadvertently drove over the little girl who had sneaked out of the house and run behind the car. The distraught man immediately called 911. Paramedics rushed the young girl to the hospital where she was pronounced dead.

Scenario Two:
Tim was recently hired by a local homebuilder to assist in construction. One afternoon the foreman asked Tim to help get the external sheathing installed on a new house before an approaching storm arrived. Tim took the initiative to pick up a high-power nail gun and began to attach sheathing materials to the house's stud frame. He had no formal training on how to use the gun, but had watched others use it. While attempting to secure the sheathing to a stud Tim misjudged the location of the stud. When he discharged the nail gun, the nail shot through the sheathing and into the head of another worker, who was killed instantly.

Scenario Three:
Joe was a sergeant in a platoon of Marines assigned to clear residences of insurgents in Fallujah, Iraq. A six-year veteran, Joe was leading his team into a compound believed to contain armed insurgents when they began taking cross-fire from an adjoining house. One of his team was hit. Joe ran over to the side of the

house next to the front door. He prepared a grenade, kicked open the door and tossed the grenade inside. After it exploded he entered the house to find a dead family in the front room. Enemy fire was actually coming from the second floor.

As you consider each of these scenarios, how did your own sense of blame vary? All of these situations are similar in that a person unintentionally made a tragic error that resulted in the death of another. However, all were very different in the degree of blame generated. In the first scenario the senator was inundated with messages of sympathy and support, both privately and in the local media. In the second scenario an OSHA investigation resulted in a citation and large fine to the homebuilder. The employee lost his job. And a civil suit was brought against both the employee and the homebuilder. In the third scenario the sergeant was court-martialed and lost his rank. Demonstrations and death threats against the Marines raged in Fallujah neighborhoods. Two other Marines later died in a booby trap set in response to this incident.

The first scenario was in a home setting and involved family, and anyone who has ever driven has had near-miss situations while backing up. It is a situation with which nearly everyone can empathize. The second scenario is set in a construction setting and involves tools most people never use. There is an expectation of competence. The situation is more foreign for most people, thus there is less empathy and a bit more blame. The third scenario is set in a war zone under enemy fire. The objective and actions (clearing a residential area) are only rarely encountered by a small percentage of people. There is an expectation of flawless execution. Few people can truly empathize with the circumstances of the moment, thus blame for the outcome is likely to be much higher. Yes, there are several other issues contributing to blame in each of these scenarios, but the varying degree of empathy is clearly a factor.

Presence at Time of (or Proximity to) Event

In Chapter 5 we will explore how causes of a problem may be far removed in time and space from the resulting effects. However, our ability to perceive relationships that bridge such metaphysical canyons is limited at best. Consequently, when a problem occurs, we look for easily identifiable causes and culprits. What this means in practical terms is those who happen to be closest to a bad event are going to be the first targets when blame is assigned.

Kids learn this at a very young age. When something bad happens they disappear from the scene - at least when they're able. In first grade I attended a small rural school. One winter day after a major snowfall the entire school was outside at lunchtime. Playground supervision was pretty much non-existent in those days. So, most of the kids were standing near the road pelting snowballs at passing cars. I stood with them, buried to my waist in a snow drift, but my limited snowball-throwing prowess prevented me from hitting the road from my position. Suddenly one of the passing cars stopped, backed up, and produced a towering sheriff's deputy from within. Everyone vanished like a breath of steam in the cold air – except the one person stuck in waist-deep snow. The deputy plucked me out of the snow bank and escorted me inside to use as a proxy of the undisciplined students as he lectured the teacher about the safety implications of our snowball battery. After the deputy left I got a personal tongue-lashing from the teacher before she re-convened the entire group for their safety lecture. I learned at age six that the person closest to "ground zero" of a bad event is likely to take the blame.

Law-abiding protesters at demonstrations occasionally get themselves arrested if some elements of the crowd become overly aggressive - simply because they were too close to the action. Even worse, in 1970 two students, who were walking past an anti-war demonstration on their way to class at Kent State University, were shot and killed by national guard troops when the demonstrators began throwing rocks and bottles. Blame and the consequences of blame are not discriminating in choosing their victims. We're all familiar with the phrase, "being in the wrong place at the wrong time." And we've all probably felt the sting of blame just for being present at the time of the event.

Crime investigators run up against this problem when they have difficulty getting witnesses to come forward. In many cases witnesses may fear being implicated or blamed in the incident because they were present at the time of the event. In the workplace, employees hope that when something goes wrong it "doesn't happen on my watch." The general wisdom is that as long as I'm not there when it happens I won't be the one to blame. Thus, even though a machine tender notices strange sounds coming from his machinery, he knows his shift ends in ten minutes. With any luck it won't break down until next shift. Surgeons know that if their patient dies due to completely unknown and unrelated complications while in surgery, they still become the prime target for the blame and litigation that is likely to follow. Or, on a more massive scale, a president of a nation realizes that if the economy can be propped up for a few more months (until the end of his term) before crashing, then his administration won't get the blame for the ensuing recession.

Popularity or Likeability of Subject

Someone who is popular or well-liked, whether that be for character traits or simply for dashing good looks, is less likely to be blamed for an event than someone who is disliked or unpleasant in some way. It's difficult to imagine a person we know and like being blamed for some kind of atrocious behavior. This raises cognitive dissonance as discussed in the previous chapter. So we look for other places to place the blame, or deny it altogether. Experienced defense attorneys want to ensure that their accused client shows up for trial clean-cut and attractive, and that the defendant attempts to make a connection with the jury. Likeability can reduce blame. Somewhat surprisingly, this reality applies even if our knowledge of a person is only through the media or their celebrity status. In 1994 O.J. Simpson, a popular actor and former football star, was arrested and tried for the murder of his ex-wife Nicole Brown Simpson and her friend Ronald Goldman. The televised trial went on for 9 months and became a national obsession. During that time those who liked Simpson could not believe he was capable of such an act, while those who didn't like him couldn't believe it when he was found not guilty. None of these people knew Simpson or knew what really happened that night. But they had all concluded that Simpson was either to blame or not. In similar fashion, in 2005, superstar Michael Jackson was accused of intoxicating and molesting a 13 year-old boy at his Neverland Ranch home. Those who loved Jackson couldn't believe this was possible. Those who didn't like Jackson couldn't believe he was found not guilty.

In June of 1862, during the early phase of America's Civil War, the Army of the Potomac, supposedly the pride of Union military might, suffered a humiliating defeat in the Peninsula Campaign. The defeat demoralized and infuriated much of the northern citizenry. General George B. McClellan was in charge of the operation and was clearly out-generaled by the Confederate leader Robert E. Lee. Yet, McClellan's dashing good looks and popularity among Union citizens helped him deflect blame for the massive failure – which cost over 15,000 Union casualties. Instead, blame landed on the unpopular and somewhat frumpy Secretary of War, Edwin Stanton. McClellan attributed the loss to Stanton's failure to provide all the resources needed to be successful. But even the New York Times saw and exposed the transference of guilt for what it was. "The first necessity of every community after a disaster is a scapegoat," reported the Times. "It is an immense relief to find some one upon whom can be fastened all the sins of a whole people, and who can then be sent into the wilderness, to be heard of no more."[49] Nonetheless, McClellan remained blame-free until repeated military failures finally revealed his lack of battle leadership skills. Even then, his admirers were outraged that he was relieved of command. If we like someone it's hard to perceive that person as blameworthy.

Degree of Media Publicity

One final note on situational factors: Our mass communications media plays a strong contributing role to our culture of blame. When a catastrophe happens (a primary subject of media reporting) a headline like *"federal agency to blame"* provides more attention-grabbing power than, *"21 contributing factors identified."* To the extent that a negative event attracts media attention, there will be an increased pressure to assign blame. If an event remains below the media radar screen it might possibly remain blame-free. However, the more newsworthy the event, the more pressure there will be to find blame. When a nuclear power plant melted down at Three Mile Island, Pennsylvania in 1979, frightening the entire world, most of the subsequent media coverage centered on finding who to blame. An enormous web of complex factors was involved, from technical instrumentation and controls, to training and supervision, to regulation and inspection, but the media primarily wanted to find someone who could be blamed.

Media clearly tries to portray any event in the most dramatic, sensational way possible. Years ago I had the misfortune to witness the fiery crash of a small twin-engine airplane with seven people on board. The media reporters were not interested in my descriptions of the developments leading up to the crash, but they continued to ask questions like, "Could you hear anyone screaming?" or "Were you close enough to see the charred bodies?" They wanted to immediately report as much gory detail as possible. In the following few days the attention turned to who was to blame. Despite a number of apparent mechanical factors, the media wanted to know about the potential pilot negligence. The more sensational the story, the more likely it will capture audience attention.

It's important to understand that for all forms of media, the survival quotient is attracting viewers or readers or listeners. And what do media consumers seem to want more than sensationalism? So, we can't blame the media for their sensationalist approach to the news. When news happens (i.e. things go wrong), the media gives their audience what they will most likely tune into. In reality, all of us individual media consumers are responsible for the type of sensationalism dished out at a media level. If we sought information and knowledge instead of entertainment and fascination from our news media, maybe blame wouldn't be so prominent.

* * * * *

Unfortunately, the presence of situational variables is usually beyond our control, even though they can significantly affect the degree of blame received in a specific incident. Not surprisingly, we have developed a range of counter-active behaviors used to defend ourselves against blame. We might deny knowledge of, or authority for an incident. We might downplay or minimize the apparent severity of problems, hopeful that some other issue grabs the spotlight before the full magnitude of our problem is revealed. Maybe we avoid being caught close to the scene of a problem to avoid guilt by association. While these behaviors are understandable, given the fickle nature of situational variables and the degree of blame they can engender, they also hurt our ability to begin to solve the underlying problems in an authentic way, and they might be as damaging as the blame itself.

5

Blame is Irrational (and distracts us from real causes)

For most, the question, "Who's to blame?" when something goes wrong seems a perfectly natural response. As we saw in the previous chapters: the cultural roots of blame run deep through much of humanity; there are many and varied psychological drivers; and numerous situational variables can amplify our likelihood of blame. We've so deeply ingrained the use of blame as a response to problems that we may be unable to imagine otherwise. Suggesting that blame is irrational might seem ludicrous at first. But in this chapter we're going to explore why blame just doesn't make much sense.

When something goes wrong, we generally conclude that someone messed up. Conventional wisdom tells us that someone, in some way, bears fault for nearly any bad event. But is it possible that most events are really too complex to attribute to one individual? What if everything that happened in life was the outcome of a complex array of forces that happened to fall together in just the right sequence to produce that outcome? Blame implies someone has control over events, but to what extent are we truly in control of things that happen? Why do things so frequently happen for seemingly inexplicable reasons?

As humans we know that we do not control the evolution of our astronomical universe (though we may aspire to influence it). We often feel we are not in control of the more immediate surrounding environment in which we function (although our influence on it is often perceptible). We may wonder, "Are we even really in control of the events and outcomes of our individual lives?" For millennia philosophers have pondered this question.

Around 350 BC Aristotle (who generally believed man was responsible for any action that was voluntary in nature) acknowledged that some things lay beyond our control. One of his more amusing observations...

> *Nobody blames a man for being ugly by nature; but we do blame those who become ugly through lack of exercise and through taking no care of their person.*[50]

On a more serious note, Aristotle went on to say that, "any discussion on matters of action cannot be more than an outline, and is bound to lack precision."[51] In other words, despite all the philosophical arguments of why people behave the way they do, sometimes we just don't know. By the late 18th century, philosophers began to contemplate the interconnectedness of events. Linear thinking, common in Western cultures, began to be challenged by an awareness of dynamic interplay more common in Eastern cultures. Friedrich Hegel proposed several perspectives on dynamics including: the whole is more than the sum of the parts, the parts cannot be understood by studying the whole, and the parts are dynamically interrelated and interdependent.[52] In the past generation, growing interest in Zen and other forms of experiential awareness have increased our recognition that life may be far more interconnected than we typically acknowledge. In his 1995 book, *Wherever You Go, There You Are*, author Jon Kabat-Zinn devotes a full chapter to consideration of "Interconnectedness," and the examination of how every event can only happen because other events have occurred that provide the right circumstances.

> *So we see the futility and the danger of letting our thinking make any thing or circumstance into an absolutely separate existence without being mindful of interconnectedness and flux. Everything is related to everything else and, in a way, simultaneously contains everything else and is contained by everything else.*[53]

In other words, everything that happens is somehow related to and driven by everything else that happens. For example, consider the following proverbial poem from the 15th century:

> *For want of a nail the shoe was lost,*
> *for want of a shoe the horse was lost,*
> *for want of a horse the knight was lost,*
> *for want of a knight the battle was lost,*
> *for want of a battle the kingdom was lost.*[54]

By the mid 20th century this notion of interconnectedness gained broad attention among the scientific community as well. In the 1940s the field of science was moving in the direction of reductionism – rapidly gaining knowledge about the small components that make up the universe, our world, even our physical bodies. Microbial, molecular, and atomic sciences were making great strides in understanding the pieces that make us who we are. But the focus was on the pieces – not necessarily how they all worked together. Biologist Ludwig Von Bertalanffy spearheaded a reaction to reductionism. He believed that science needed to emphasize the interaction of components with each other and with their environment – in other words, looking at the forest, or perhaps even the whole ecosystem, instead of just the trees.[55] Von Bertalanffy's push to look at the whole picture is widely recognized as the genesis of what has come to be called systems theory.

During World War II an early systems theorist, mathematician Norbert Wiener, who worked at conceptualizing automated communication and control systems for the American military, laid the groundwork for what would ultimately become known as the field of Cybernetics. Later, in the 1950s, several individuals including W. Ross Ashby and W. Grey Walter advanced Wiener's concepts to formalize and promote Cybernetics.[56] Cybernetics is based on the view that all systems are governed by complex, circular feedback mechanisms that shape the direction and evolution of those systems. In essence, any event generates information or feedback to its encompassing system, which, in turn, adjusts or adapts to that event and responds with new events.

This notion shifted scientific thinking. Instead of viewing past linear causes as the determinant of actions, we began to see systems as dynamic, living organisms that generated their own actions geared towards a future state. The concept has been demonstrated in all kinds of systems from electro-mechanical, to natural, to social.

In the 1970s, systems theory reached a more popular level as it began to be incorporated into both science and social studies at colleges and universities. The application of systems theory to global perspectives led to a better understanding of human impact on our planet. One of those focused on large-scale applications of systems theory was Jay Forrester, a founding member of the Club of Rome – an organization of academic and political leaders of the day. In 1972 the Club of Rome published a watershed report called *Limits to Growth*, [57] which essentially said that if we keep doing what we're doing now (pollution, resource consumption, overpopulation) the world would exceed its capacity in the foreseeable future with catastrophic consequences for mankind.[58] Once again it was the interconnectedness of events that was driving the system, not individual specific actions. Forrester also commented on our myopia in dealing with human behavior.

> *Human experience...leads us to look close to the symptoms of trouble for a cause. But when we look, we are misled because the social system presents us with an apparent cause that is plausible according to the lessons we have learned from simple systems, although this apparent cause is usually a coincident occurrence that, like the symptom itself, is being produced by the feedback-loop dynamics of a larger system.*[59]

Forrester's comments begin to illustrate why blame may be an irrational response to unwanted events. In blame we search close to the symptom to find the cause of the problem (i.e. the culprit's erroneous ways). But that apparent cause (culprit's action) is likely only another part of the feedback-response loop of the broader system. The action we are blaming is probably just a coincident occurrence driven by all the interacting dynamics of the system.

Systems thinking involves looking at the whole picture – how all the components of a system interact with each other and their environment. What systems theorists recognize is that those interactions are incredibly complex with varying amounts of feedback, randomness, patterns, and chaos all playing integral roles. No one component or action within the system is the primary cause of any outcome, but rather the interplay among components creates the outcome. While removing or changing any one component may alter or eliminate the outcome, that one component on its own could not have created the outcome without all the other contributing components.

In late 2004, after the Bush-Kerry Presidential race, an article appeared in Wyoming's *Casper Star-Tribune* headlined, "Blame air conditioning for Kerry loss."[60] The author, James Wiley, a Fellow of the American Geographical Society and Associate Professor of Geography, offered a tongue-in-cheek systems perspective on the election outcome. Wiley pointed out that since the invention of air-conditioning in the 1940s U.S. population (and corresponding Electoral College votes) has shifted from traditionally Democratic states like New York, Pennsylvania, Illinois, Massachusetts, and Michigan to states that tend to vote Republican like Florida, Texas, Arizona, Georgia, and Nevada. Without air conditioning this shift would not have taken place and the increased Electoral votes from northern states would have placed John Kerry in the White House. Is this perspective a simple amusement or accurate analysis? Certainly the invention of air conditioning on its own did not give George Bush a second term as President, but would changing that one component have changed the outcome of the system? It's possible.

One of the most fascinating observations of systems theory is that the contributing causes of any condition may be far removed in both time and space from the outcome. This bears repeating… *contributing causes of any condition may be far removed in both time and space from the outcome.* Many of us have contemplated how a simple change in actions at one point in our past might have led to a completely different life today.

Had Fred gone to the ball game instead of stopping at his friend's party that night, he would not have met Jane, who he ultimately married. Because Jane was from California, Fred moved there with her and completed his engineering degree at Berkeley. In the engineering program he met a couple of other bright individuals with whom he started a computer firm after graduation. They became enormously successful, which allowed Fred and Jane to devote large amounts of money and time to charitable causes and help thousands of other people. Now the systems question is: if Fred had gone to the ball game instead of the party, how dramatically different might things be today for those recipients of his charity work? Was his decision to go to his friend's party the cause of his success? Not exactly. But it was a critical component to the ultimate outcome. And that illustrates the dynamics of systems. One action rarely, if ever, causes an outcome – but merely contributes to the result. Yet, alter that one action – even far removed in time and space - and the outcome could be totally different.

A similar premise was classically portrayed in the 1946 Frank Capra movie *It's a Wonderful Life*. George Baily (played by Jimmy Stewart) is about to leap off a bridge because, despite his best efforts, the money needed to keep his Building and Loan business afloat was lost and he is in a state of drunken despair. Besides, many of his life's ambitions have gone unmet. However, at the last moment George's guardian angel steps in and takes George on a visionary voyage to see the gruesome picture of what life in Bedford Falls would have been like if George had never been born. This time the systems question is: had George not been born, and Bedford Falls ended up as the dark village of Pottersville, who would have been to blame? Would George's parents be at fault?

The concept of contributory causal actions being far removed in time and space is commonly illustrated by a concept known as the Butterfly Effect. Through the technology of computer modeling, meteorologists have shown how minute actions in one part of the globe can potentially create enormous weather variances later on in another part of the world. At a 1972 conference of the American Association for the Advancement of Science Philip Merilees presented the topic, *Does the flap of a butterfly's wings in Brazil set off a tornado in Texas?*[61] While that kind of linkage seems preposterous to most people, it is the bread and butter of systems thinking.

The outcomes for which we blame people are also the result of complex systems. Actions, events, or influences that may have happened long ago or far away could be critical components to the outcome we are blaming. Remove or alter that one component and our culprit might not have committed the offending action. Knowledgeable parents, teachers, and leaders from all walks of life understand that their own words, or displays of behavior, can influence decisions and actions of others long into the future. And this influence can be negative as well as positive. A cavalier statement by a parent to a young child about drug use could be the tipping factor 10 years later in that teenager's decision to experiment with drug use. Remove that one statement (or alter any of dozens of other factors) and the teen's decision may have gone the other way. So who is to blame for the teenager's drug use? If a business owner brags to employees about depreciating his new Mercedes Benz as a business expense on his taxes (even though it is obviously only used for personal use), what influence might that have on the bookkeeper's decision a few years later to "fudge the numbers" and put a few extra bucks into his own pocket? Who's to blame for the embezzlement?

A number of years ago John Stossel, correspondent for ABC News, presented an example of this kind of remote linkage. His report was focused on how our sense of risk is often misplaced and he used a systemic example to illustrate his point. In 1989 the CBS program *60 Minutes* had raised alarm when it dramatized the risk of cancer from an agricultural chemical called Alar, used to prevent damage to apple crops. The report implied that Alar was a significant threat to anyone who ate apples or drank apple juice from orchards treated with the chemical. Later responses from The World Health Organization, the American Medical Association, and the U.S. Surgeon General refuted these claims,[62] but by then, apple growers had suffered millions of dollars in lost sales. Stossel questioned what kinds of alternative risks could conceivably be generated when we overact against small risks. His hypothetical chain of systemic linkages went something like this...

To eliminate an unsubstantiated health risk from its application on apples, the FDA banned Alar. The ban meant that apple farmers would now need to undertake more labor intensive means to control insects, and that crop yields would likely go down. The increased costs of production and lower yields would translate into higher prices of apples to the consumer. As you increase the cost of food staples (like apples) you disproportionately increase the economic pressures on the poor. As the economic pressures increase, some number of poverty-sticken people who are at the margins of survival will be driven to desperate measures such as prostitution or drug trafficking to afford food. Increased prostitution and drug trafficking leads to a natural increase in the spread of AIDS. So while the FDA action was intended to reduce health risks, it may have inadvertently contributed to an even greater health risk. Moreover, to carry the systems thinking even further, if the increase in AIDS cases causes a large chemical company to divert R&D resources from agricultural pesticides to AIDS treatments, then the whole cycle may continue to escalate.

Is this notion far-fetched? Only if you assume a linear correlation at each step in the system. While the single act of banning Alar may or may not have had a measurable effect on the incidence of AIDS, the reality is that hundreds of such factors are at work at any moment in time influencing the incidence of AIDS. And it is the systemic interaction of all those factors that really drives the outcome. Remember, any action may be influenced by antecedents that are far removed in time and space. And that action may, in turn, have subsequent influences also far removed in time and space.

The same linkages are at work when we seek to blame someone for an outcome that is intricately tied into a larger system. Although we like to simplify the motivations to human actions, most acts (whether glorious or disastrous) are driven by complex interacting circumstances, not simple willful or careless decisions.

After the first Gulf War, Iraqi President Saddam Hussein engaged in ruthless persecution of the Kurds in the north of Iraq. To minimize the conflict & facilitate humanitarian aid, a "no-fly" zone was established north of the 36th parallel. Iraqi flights were not allowed in this airspace. To prevent Iraqi incursions and manage the authorized air traffic in that area, a complex management and enforcement system was put in place. It included:
- Daily air tasking orders that detailed flight plans in the area
- Airborne radar and control centers known as AWACS
- Patrol flights by US fighter jets to intercept and deal with incursions
- On-board technologies for the identification of other aircraft

On the morning of April 14, 1994 a large group of high-level peacekeeping staff including Turks, Brits, French, Kurds, and Americans, all stationed in Turkey, boarded two US Blackhawk helicopters. Their itinerary included a visit to the military command center in Zakhu, Iraq, then unannounced visits to several field destinations. To avoid leaking information about this high-level security visit, no flight plan was filed with the day's Air Tasking Order. From Turkey to Zakhu the helicopters maintained radio contact with the AWACS control center. However, upon departing Zakhu for the field destinations, the plan was simply, "radio silence and fly low."

About 7:20 a.m. the first American fighter patrol of the day arrived in the area. Based on the day's Air Tasking Order the two F-15 pilots expected to be the first "friendly" aircraft in the area. However, upon reaching their patrol zone, they made radar contact with low-flying, unknown aircraft. The pilots contacted AWACS which confirmed the sighting, but had no identification on the target. AWACS controllers instructed the F-15 pilots to make a high-speed intercept pass of the target for visual identification. The pilots made two passes, but with the morning sun just rising and the helicopters in the shadows of the hills, the F-15 pilots thought the helicopters were Russian-made Hinds, which were used by the Iraqi forces, instead of American Blackhawks.

The pilots then checked for identification of the helicopters using a transmission system called "Identification Friend or Foe" (IFF). Receivers on the F-15s would recognize the code programmed into the transponders on the helicopters. The helicopter flight was not transmitting the code assigned for the day, and it did not register the correct code in another "automatic" mode.

Finally, the pilots contacted AWACS again for instructions and were given authorization to fire on the targets. A few moments later both Blackhawks had been destroyed by air-to-air missiles. All 26 people on board were killed.[63]

As might be expected, politicians and the media were quick to begin the hunt for blame. Senator James Exon was quoted in USA Today: "I have to think this is something that's going to cause some heads to roll." Then Speaker of the House, Newt Gingrich, shot blame a different direction: "It's a symptom I think of the decay that has set in because the Clinton defense budgets are simply much too low."[64] The Senate Armed Services Committee, which had a scheduled hearing the following day to discuss lessons learned during the Gulf War, quickly turned their discussion to the incident.[65] Most members were somewhat restrained on assigning blame just yet, but it was clear to Gen. Larry Henry, Air Force deputy chief of staff, that answers needed to be coming fast. He assured the committee that U.S. pilots flying over Iraq were not "cowboys or trigger-happy."[66]

Meanwhile, according to Time magazine, an un-named Pentagon official did question whether the fighter jocks' adrenaline overrode their judgment. "I'm sure the F-15 pilots said, *'There's something there—let's get it!'*... I'm sure they had their fangs out," said the official.[67] Newspaper editorials across the country demanded answers. Under enormous pressure to find out who was at fault for this tragedy, Defense Secretary William Perry pledged to discipline anyone found to be negligent.[68] But as details of the incident emerged, deciding whose head should roll became increasingly fuzzy.

After the full investigation had concluded, Perry, in summarizing the official report, indicated that the accident was a

result of, "errors, omissions, and procedures," and that four primary factors were the most significant:
- The F-15 pilots' mis-identification of the Blackhawks
- The failure of the AWACS crew to properly intervene
- The lack of integration of the helicopters' flight into the Air Tasking Order
- The technical failure of the IFF system.

However, the report listed over 100 actual contributing factors to the accident.[69] Nonetheless, media and politicians continued to attribute blame to whoever, in their judgment, had messed up and deserved to be punished.

Over time the incident continued to receive scrutiny. Lt. Col Scott Snook, himself a victim of friendly fire and a Ph.D. in organizational behavior, conducted an extensive sociological investigation of the accident that culminated in his book, *Friendly Fire*, published in 2000. According to Snook's exhaustive research and analysis, there was no individual culprit in this event. Instead, the outcome was predictable. In the book, Snook lays out an integrated model of all the various inter-related factors that led to the ultimate shoot-down of the helicopters. Who's to blame for the tragic consequence? According to Snook, the dynamics of the system were the cause, not individual actions.[70]

In the workplace, where blame is ubiquitous, systems are highly interconnected and complex. Few people understood the futility of blame in the workplace better than W. Edwards Deming, a mathematician and business consultant who is credited with having turned Japan's post-war manufacturing sector into a world leader in quality and productivity. Deming felt that the prevailing focus on individual worker shortcomings, especially failures to meet quotas and performance targets, demonstrated management's ignorance of the larger system. Deming abhorred many common management practices such as motivational slogans and posters, arbitrary improvement goals, individual merit pay, and performance appraisals because they all ignored the impact of the system in determining the actions of individuals. According to Deming, individual performance, both positive and negative, was far more defined by the vagaries of the system than by any personal value or vice. In commenting about a company that had implemented a program to reward the top production employee of the month (lowest defect rate) he said:

> *There is no harm in a lottery, so far as I know, provided it is called a lottery. To call it an award of merit when the selection is merely a lottery, however, is to demoralize the whole force, prize winners included. Everybody will suppose that there are good reasons for the selection and will be trying to explain and reduce differences between men. This would be a futile exercise when the only differences are random deviations...*[71]

Deming believed that the aim of leadership was "not to find and record failures of men, but to remove the causes of failure."[72] If someone made a mistake, management's role was not to blame the individual, but to find out how the system failed.

> *The performance of anybody is the result of a combination of many forces – the person himself, the people that he works with, the job, the material he works on, his equipment, his customer, his management, his supervision, environmental conditions (noise, confusion, poor food in the company's cafeteria).*[73]

Once one begins to understand the complex chain of factors that leads to any outcome, then that person will also begin to realize that blame is irrational. As Forrester pointed out, when things go wrong we look too close to the symptom for our cause, and most often the identified cause is simply a coincident occurrence. The real cause might be far removed in both time and space. Blame also ignores the complexity of the system, which generally exceeds the capacity of human thinking at the moment individual decisions are made. Only with the advantage of retrospect can we often see why an individual act was the wrong choice. Blame distracts us from finding and solving the real problems, and it comes with collateral costs as illustrated in Chapter 1. Blame assumes we control our lives, our environment, and our universe. But understanding of systems theory shows that events are much more the result of interconnected occurrences.

Why don't we take more of a systems perspective on understanding problems? Probably because systems thinking is not natural for us. We tend to think in a linear fashion – if A, then B. Especially when problems arise, we want simple, clean, easy-to-understand, black-and-white answers. (Who messed up, and who is going to take the fall?) This is perhaps less a chastisement of human nature than of our educational development. Our educational system devotes very little attention to understanding the complexity of systems that envelope our world. Instead we are taught to think in a very linear fashion. We don't think about systemic influences because we haven't been taught to think that way. And if our knowledge of systems theory is limited, our ability to effectively solve problems is going to be severely curtailed. When the level of complexity in a problem begins to exceed our comprehension, we default back to our habitual process of finding a scapegoat and assigning blame.

If one accepts a systems perspective on life, then blame becomes irrational. So, is it possible that nobody is really to blame for anything? Before you try to answer that question (or object to it entirely) let's consider how blame differs from accountability or personal responsibility.

6

Blame, Accountability, and Personal Responsibility

If it feels good, do it!
Pop mantra of the 60s

By now you're probably crying out, "But, what about personal responsibility for one's actions?" Do the arguments on systemic causes imply that anything goes? Even if all outcomes and events are driven by myriad interconnected factors, don't people still do unacceptable things? If someone shows up consistently late for work, has an extra-marital affair, robs a convenience store, or murders another, are we not right to blame the person? If we don't blame people for their wrong doings, how do we maintain social order? How do we run a business? How do we extract justice? The answer to these questions lies in clarifying our understanding of the differences among blame, accountability, and personal responsibility.

In everyday use we have blurred the distinctions among these concepts. We talk about "holding someone accountable" when we're actually blaming them for something gone wrong. We exhort organizational or cultural values like "enforcement of personal responsibility" that do little, other than promote scapegoating. Moreover, the codification and prosecution of culpability through our legal system has further confused common understanding of the distinctions. But the differences among blame, accountability, and personal responsibility are far more than semantic! This chapter will construct some operational definitions for these terms and illustrate the importance of clearly differentiating among them.

Blame versus Accountability

Appreciating how any act or event interconnects with, and influences, nearly everything else helps us understand why things happen, and vaporizes much justification for blame. But does that also suggest there should be no consequences to one's actions? For any society, organization, or family to survive for any length of time, it must define behaviors that are needed for sustenance; and, it must define behaviors that are detrimental to its existence. Accordingly, we construct compensation and reward systems for behaviors we desire, and impose penalties for behaviors that are contrary to our purpose. Willful, wanton acts of damage, havoc, or deceit must be controlled to prevent chaos in society. The person who puts a gun in your face and demands your wallet must face a sufficient deterrent or the behavior would become unpleasantly commonplace. And even less-intentional wrong-doings often warrant appropriate consequences. If an air traffic controller seems to have a problem keeping his targets properly identified, then we certainly want the person removed from the job until the source of the problem can be identified and corrected.

For starters, let us distinguish between *blame* for *outcomes*, and *accountability* for *actions*. If your wallet is stolen at gunpoint (clearly a bad outcome) you will feel violated and angry. Your sense of righteousness will demand justice. To you, the robber is a bad guy, perhaps completely evil. You desperately hope that he is captured and sentenced to prison. In short, you'll blame the robber without having a complete picture of why your wallet was taken at gunpoint (the bad outcome). But if we take a systems perspective we should be asking, "What kinds of contributing factors may have led to this bad outcome?"

Suppose the robber's wife recently passed away after a long illness, leaving him with medical bills that forced a bankruptcy. Taking care of her and their two young children cost him his job. Their home was repossessed, and he and the kids are now living in a cardboard box under an overpass. He needed money because they were all going hungry, and he couldn't face taking the kids downtown again tomorrow to beg on the street corner. Would you still blame him? If you knew his story, you might willingly have given him the money in your wallet.

And what about your contributing factors to this bad outcome? Why were you walking through that seedy area of town late at night without sufficient accompaniment to discourage attack? What personal actions made you appear an easy target?

What about the other systemic factors? Why did the robber not have sufficient healthcare insurance to cover his wife's illness? What dynamics occurred at his place of employment to cause him to lose his job? Did the company offer appropriate assistance to help him through his personal struggles? Does the community provide aid to the homeless that might have kept his family off the street until he could regain employment? A simple change in any of these factors (or untold others) could have short-circuited the bad outcome you encountered.

None of this absolves the robber of accountability for his *action* of taking your wallet at gunpoint. We'll get to that shortly. But the *outcome* of your stolen wallet goes well beyond the robber's actions. And *blaming* the robber for that outcome is oversimplifying the problem, and perpetuating a dysfunctional way of thinking.

Blame involves the transference of responsibility away from ourselves and onto some other person (or even onto an animal or inanimate object). Blame typically implies a value judgment. It suggests that a moral imperative has been violated, that the culprit is bad or evil in some way, and that punishment must follow. Through the act of blaming, the blamer feels endowed with a degree of righteousness or moral superiority over the blamed. Blame connotes the administration of "justice" – that right has prevailed over wrong. Finally, assignment of blame brings with it a false sense of problem resolution – the culprit has been identified and should be dispatched appropriately. And, since the culprit is the problem, all will now be well.

Accountability, on the other hand, is all about consequences for *actions*, regardless of *outcomes*. Consequences are a natural and logical part of our physical world, and we learn about them early. If you drop your pacifier out of the crib, you can no longer reach it. If you stick your finger in the lighted birthday candles, it hurts. If you go to school without your coat in winter, you get very cold (but at least you look cool). Nature holds you accountable, without prejudice or judgment, for these actions. The consequences are predictable and consistent.

We also create consequences in our societal, organizational, and family structures for actions we deem unacceptable. The driver who exceeds the speed limit is subject to a traffic citation (even if no accident occurred). The employee who routinely fails to report to work on time will likely lose his job (even if all the work got done). The teenager who stays out past curfew finds himself grounded for a week (even though the late arrival caused no bad outcome).

Fact: Actions have consequences.

Corollary: Consequences modify actions. They do so most effectively when: (a) predetermined and known, and (b) consistently applied – just like in nature.

We should think of *accountability* as the steadfast application of these pre-determined consequences for behaviors that are naturally, socially, organizationally, or personally unacceptable. Pure accountability remains free from value judgment and vindictiveness. When holding someone accountable for *actions*, you remain cognizant that the causes of any associated bad *outcome* may be far removed in time and space, and likely involve a mass of interwoven factors. You may understand that the offender had rational reasons for the action. You may even acknowledge your own degree of contribution to the outcome.

Even if we understand the motives of the robber who took your wallet, even if we acknowledge the many other contributing factors to that outcome, his actions are still unacceptable in our society. If caught, he will be held accountable for them. The judge doesn't need to blame the guy. In fact, the judge can acknowledge the contributory circumstances to the action, and has some latitude in assigning consequences based on the facts of the case. Accountability can be had without blame. Attribution of blame will do nothing to solve future robberies. Nor will it solve this person's plight, or the underlying problem of homelessness and desperation in our society that led to the holdup. So what's the point of blaming? Yet, the cultural, psychological, and situational variables covered in prior chapters will certainly drive us toward blaming the robber for our bad outcome.

Likewise, the air traffic controller mentioned above must be held accountable for his errors – we can't afford to have airliners colliding with one another. But the potential causes for the problem could be manifest, so blame is unwarranted and unhelpful. Yet, if his errors result in an aircraft collision, he will certainly face tremendous blame for the high profile outcome.

Consequence Enforcer versus Blamer

Part of the reason blame is so rampant in our society is that we fail to differentiate between "Consequence Enforcer" and "Blamer." So, it's worth restating four principles of accountability.

First, consequences for undesirable behaviors should be *predetermined*. In families, in organizations, and in society, we know what kinds of behaviors are not conducive to our common interests. Consequences for those behaviors should be determined ahead of time, at least to a reasonable extent. Without such prior knowledge, the behavior modification value of consequences diminishes dramatically. If a teenager does not know that coming home after curfew will lead to grounding, there is little incentive to leave the party before others have left.

Second, consequences work best when consistently applied. If a high school teacher routinely ignores students who are engaged on their smart phones during class, then one time suddenly and angrily confiscates poor Jason's phone, Jason will feel victimized, and the other students will slowly return to playing on their phones once the immediate threat has passed. In contrast, the small village of Rosendale, Wisconsin so consistently enforces its 25 mph speed zone, that the only violators are those from outside the area who are unaware of the strict enforcement. Consistent application of the rule means very few speeders.

Third, consequences should be based on the undesirable *action*, and independent of *outcome*. We know that the *action* of distracted driving leads to many traffic deaths each year. But the consequences are often tied to the *outcome* instead of the action. A driver who is texting and scrapes a barrier where a construction worker was standing minutes ago might incur no consequence other than a paint blemish on the car. However, had the construction worker been in that spot a few minutes later, he would have been hit and killed, and the driver would likely receive a lengthy prison sentence for negligent homicide. In both cases, the driver's decisions and actions were identical. Yet, for some reason, we assign consequences based on the *outcome*, which is determined largely by random factors outside the driver's control. If we sincerely want to deter distracted driving, serious consequences should be based on the *action* of distracted driving, not the *outcome* of an injured person.

Fourth, the application of consequences should be free from emotional influence and value judgment. When something goes wrong, subsequent feelings of victimization, or a demand for "justice," or a sense of moral superiority, are clear signs that blame is happening. Those types of feelings drive a desire for more severe consequences than what may make sense given the actions of the wrong-doer.

"I didn't mean to do it."

What about intent? Should unintentional acts incur the same consequence as intentional ones? Once again, we need to ask whether we're focusing on *outcomes* or *actions*. Most people don't intend to cause bad outcomes. Sure, there are the exceptions – the psychopath murderers, the jihadist terrorists, those bent on revenge, and the like, who truly want to produce a bad outcome. But most of the time, when something goes wrong, the outcome was unintended. And, as discussed above, accountability consequences should never be based on outcomes.

Actions, however, are mostly intended, and follow some kind of conscious or unconscious decision-making process. Aside from completely involuntary actions, like tripping and knocking over Grandma's prized Tiffany lamp, most of our actions are intentional. And intentional actions do warrant appropriate consequences. But if our objective is to curtail future undesirable actions, then we also need to give consideration to the developmental aspect of behavior modification. People who act in ways that are detrimental to our family, our organization, or our society, may simply lack a full understanding of the impact of their actions. In family and organizational settings, one four-step developmental model that works quite well in achieving compliance with desired actions goes something like this.

Step One: Is the person aware of the expected behavior? If not, clarify the expectation.

Step Two: Is the person capable of complying with the expectation? If not, then that capacity needs to be developed, or else the expectation must be modified.

Step Three: If knowledge and capacity exist, does the person understand the social or organizational rationale for the expectation? If not, provide that understanding.

Step Four: Does the person know the personal consequences of failure to comply with the expectation? If not, make those consequences known.

Having proceeded through all four steps, application of consequences is completely warranted.

A Note on Personal Responsibility

Personal responsibility can best be described as the *intrinsic* side of accountability. Whereas consequences are imposed upon someone externally, personal responsibility is the understanding and acceptance of how my actions have been incompliant with expectations, or how they have in some way contributed to an unfavorable outcome. Because of its intrinsic nature, you can't force personal responsibility upon someone. Either they "get it" or they don't. It goes back to the systemic nature of things.

If I drive a gas-guzzler (or any vehicle for that matter), I contribute to oil drilling and transport, and ultimately, to oil-soaked pelicans. If I rely on paid political ads in determining for whom to vote, I contribute to ineffective government, and ultimately, to domestic and international problems. If I live a "couch-potato" existence, I contribute to dismal national health statistics, and ultimately, to skyrocketing healthcare costs.

When you understand personal responsibility in this light, you are less likely to play the blame game, and are better positioned to participate in the administration of consequences for the actions of others. Failure to see our own connection to a problem sets us up for blaming.

In fact, the central paradox of blame is that the act of blaming is actually the abdication of personal responsibility. By blaming, I shift responsibility for the event away from me, and onto you. Just as the ancient Hebrews shifted their collective sins onto the unfortunate sacrificial goat, and thereby cleansed the people of the community, blame shifts my share of culpability for an event onto a sacrificial person or object, and thereby cleanses me of responsibility.

In a complex systemic problem, (take any of the school shooting incidents of the past few years for example) lots of people have some contributory responsibility. The shooters planned and carried out their actions, so their contributory responsibility is obvious. But what about other players? Did students who belittled and isolated the shooters for months prior have any contributory responsibility? Had they not done so, the shooters may never have acted. Did the parents of the shooters play a role by not sensing the degree of emotional disturbance in their children? Did the school boards and administrations play a role by not providing the type of guidance that would have encouraged the shooters to seek help, or by not creating a more secure facility? Did teachers overlook the dynamics of harassment going on in front of them? Did friends of the shooters support and feed their hostility? Did police respond in the best tactical fashion to minimize casualties? Did legislators (and the voters who elected them) influence this event through laws or policy? One might even ask: if the victims had responded differently, could the outcome have been altered? All of the people involved potentially had some contributory impact on (personal responsibility for) each of the tragedies. Many interventions could have short-circuited the final outcome. But by scapegoating and blaming a select few, we absolve ourselves of our own personal responsibility for contributing to the event.

An even darker reality is that blame is actually a game of victimization. When something goes wrong we feel the pain (hurt, offense, embarrassment, delay, financial setback, insult, shock, obstruction). While we could step back, think about the systemic causes of that pain, and contemplate our own personal responsibility for the outcome, an easier, and more emotionally decadent response, is to feel victimized. "I've been hurt, and someone needs to pay." Once we've taken that step, our self-righteousness kicks in and a lust for perceived "justice" begins to take over. We all relate to the John Wayne movie where right prevails over evil, and the bad guy gets his just dessert. If we can find a culprit for our problem, and teach him a lesson, then we've gotten retribution and our hurt has been soothed. Blame supplants personal responsibility. Unfortunately, this victim/blame response is so common, and so deeply entrenched into our thinking and behavior, that it dominates a large portion of our energy and efforts in society, our organizations, and our relationships.

Consider this: of the 145 million people in the U.S. workforce, over 1 million are attorneys.[74] There are 750,000 ranchers and farmers who grow things. There are 500,000 truck drivers who move things. There are 233,000 architects who design our living and work spaces. But we need more than a million attorneys to deal with legal concerns. In all fairness, we live in a complex society, so development and interpretation of all the rules, and protection of our various rights, is a big job. But we all know that victimization-fueled blame, channeled through our tort system, consumes far too many social resources. Each year an organization called The Michigan Lawsuit Abuse Watch holds a contest and awards recognition for the wackiest warning labels that have resulted from lawsuits predicated on victimization and its abdication of personal responsibility.[75] When a five-inch fishing lure with three large steel hooks requires a label that reads, "Harmful if swallowed," or when a washing machine at a Laundromat requires a label that reads, "Do not put any person in this washer," or when a baby stroller requires a label that reads, "Remove child before folding," then we have evidence that our tort system coddles those who wish to abdicate personal responsibility in favor of blame.

When someone in authority, like a manager, blames a subordinate for a failure, the intention may be to "enforce personal responsibility." But in reality, the manager ends up submitting himself as the victim, and thus, surrenders his real power to affect a solution for the problem. Moreover, the attempt to transfer personal responsibility to the employee is futile. It just doesn't work that way. Most likely, the employee is already keenly aware of what role he or she played in the bad event, and also that there were many other contributing factors that led to the outcome. Some ostentatious flogging will not spur the employee to accept a greater degree of responsibility for the event. But if you try to force someone to "take personal responsibility" you will likely just frustrate yourself. Better that you spend your time considering your own systemic contribution to the event. That is something you can control.

To Summarize

While blaming someone (or something) for a bad *outcome* is irrational due to the many systemic factors, and dysfunctional because it take our eye off the real underlying causes, holding someone accountable for their *actions* with predetermined and consistent consequences is necessary for an orderly society.

The distinction between blame for outcomes, and accountability for actions, can be confusing at first. We are not taught to recognize that distinction. But the more you begin to look for the difference, the better you will get at spotting it.

Case Study: Myrtle and Ethel

Let's consider blame versus accountability in a common workplace situation. Myrtle and Ethel worked in the shipping department of Nuts-n-Bolts, an industrial parts supplier. Their job was to pull, verify, pack, and ship customer orders. Both were in their mid 60s and lived alone. Neither had accumulated any significant retirement assets, so they worked this job to supplement their minimal Social Security payments. The physical routine took its toll in daily aches and pains on both women, but besides needing the income, they both enjoyed the camaraderie in the shipping department. One day Myrtle and Ethel got a little too chatty (Myrtle's granddaughter found a new lover and wanted to leave her current abusive boyfriend). During the discussion, the overnight shipping label for the Excelsior order was mistakenly affixed to the box with the Acme order (which was also overnight) and vice-versa, and the boxes were shipped to the wrong destinations.

Next day, the production manager at Excelsior was livid when the wrong order arrived. He had a machine down waiting for the parts, and had promised his own customers immediate deliveries once he got things back up and running. Now he would have to wait another day for the parts and his customers would be very angry. This wasn't his first problem with Nuts-n-Bolts either. He previously ran into back-order problems on two occasions, and was billed incorrectly on another. He called the general manager back at Nuts-n-Bolts and said he was finding a new supplier. Immediately following the phone call, Nuts-n-Bolt's general manager called the shipping manager into his office and said, "Joe, are you and your department just a bunch of bone-heads? You're obviously not concerned about the welfare of this company. You've had repeated screw-ups, but I don't see anyone being disciplined. You don't seem to have a sense of urgency about customer service. You need to 'can' whoever was responsible for this latest mess and send the message to the rest of your team that screw-ups will not be tolerated. If you don't put the fear of God in your team, I will."

Joe was very discouraged. In both of the back-order incidents, his inventory clerk had followed all the right procedures. Re-stock orders were placed when the part hit its designated order level. In the first case the domestic part manufacturer had gone on strike the day the order was placed. The inventory clerk took good initiative to locate and source product from a European producer, but it took an extra week for delivery. In the second case the parts were shipped on time from a Chinese producer, but the container with the order was lost overboard during trans-oceanic shipment. Again, the inventory clerk responded brilliantly to replace the lost order. But in both cases Excelsior had placed abnormally large part orders that had depleted Nuts-n-Bolt's inventory and run into back-order situations. The billing error resulted when Excelsior ordered, then cancelled, then re-ordered the same part all in one week. The original billing was processed on the last day of the month. And the cancellation and subsequent billing rolled into a new month so the corrected invoice didn't arrive at Excelsior for 30 days. This latest "screw-up" – Ethel and Myrtle – was plain human error. But they had been reliable workers for the past 3 years, and never complained about the undesirable working conditions. Now they were supposed to become the scapegoats for the loss of the Excelsior account. Joe knew it would be tough to replace them with anyone better.

That evening Joe called a friend over at a large auto parts distribution center who invited him to come to work for them. Next morning Joe went in to Nuts-n-Bolts early, cleared out his desk, and left an e-mail for the general manager that he would not be returning.

Variations on this scenario are played out hundreds of times each day in workplaces throughout the world. Individuals are blamed for complex problems that would have been impossible to predict and correct ahead of time. They are judged as incompetent, careless, lazy, or lacking in some other moral quality. But blame never cures the problem, and rarely has any long-term, beneficial effect in eliminating the undesired contributory actions from the system in which in was generated. In this case a bad outcome (loss of Excelsior contract) is being tagged to a few specific incidents, most immediately, the packaging mistake. However, there are many contributing factors that led up to the ultimate outcome – many of which are outside of Nuts-n-Bolt's realm of control. Blame serves absolutely no real good in this situation (although it provides the blamer with a misguided sense that the problem has been addressed).

What about accountability? Loss of a key customer is not something most companies can tolerate repeatedly. Where does accountability lie in this case? That is a much more difficult question to answer. Are we talking accountability for the outcome, or accountability for specific actions? Clearly Myrtle and Ethel should be held accountable for their packaging mistake. Conversations should not be so involved as to result in distraction from work tasks. Appropriate consequences for such a first-time mistake might be awareness training of how their actions contributed to the loss of a customer. Myrtle and Ethel likely had no prior appreciation for the potential impact of their actions, and will feel horrible when they find out what happened. But they are not solely accountable for the loss of the customer.

Joe was accountable for the "systems" of the shipping department. As such he might have influenced the outcome by increasing the minimum inventory levels of parts, but space availability and increased holding costs would have been affected. He could have better trained Myrtle and Ethel on possible impacts of shipping errors. So, consequences for his portion of accountability might involve conducting a formal analysis of operations to identify future potential sources of shipping errors.

Not mentioned in the scenario, Nuts-n-Bolts' sales or customer service team is accountable for maintaining a good relationship with Excelsior. They could have been keeping tighter communication with Excelsior to understand the developing anger and defusing it with clear explanations of what Nuts-n-Bolts was doing to resolve those concerns. Consequences for their portion of accountability might be assignment to visit all key accounts in the next 30 days and provide a formal report on levels of customer satisfaction.

The general manager is accountable for the overall functioning of Nuts-n-Bolts. He could have been working with all departments to identify potential customer satisfaction problems and building a culture of connection to the company's customers. Consequences for his portion of accountability might involve a reduction in annual bonus proportionate to the loss of profits attributable to Excelsior's departure.

All of these players could be held accountable for their contribution to the problem without any degree of the value judgment that accompanies blame. Systems are complex. Stuff happens. Accountability can be defined and addressed appropriately and rationally without blame. The difference between blame and accountability is not a nuance of semantics, but a wholesale difference in perspective, belief systems, and response to problems. Accountability is critical in all societies. But we must be on guard that the enforcement of accountability is not little more than thinly disguised blame.

7

Reducing Blame

If no one ever again asked, "Who's to Blame?" the world would be a markedly better place in which to live. Families would become more disposed to work toward collective ends, and relationships of all kinds would become more harmonious. Workplaces would become more productive and creative as fear and reservation were replaced with engagement and creativity. Perhaps even government gridlock could be traded for constructive progress on social issues. (Those few who profit from blame - ambulance chasers and the like - might lose out in the short term, but would probably be better off in the long run with a different line of work.) While the realities of humanity may make the vision of a blame-free world a bit Utopian, there is little doubt we have the capability to make a perceptible dent in the negative impacts blame has on our lives. This chapter outlines several steps we can take to reduce our obsession with blame.

Before we step off in this direction however, we must each ask ourselves a blatant and honest question: "Do I really want to stop blaming others?" Remember, blame is like a psychological narcotic that allows us to feel good in the face of things gone wrong. The ability to validate our own moral and culpable righteousness offers a potent elixir, when the alternative could mean facing up to our contributory accountability and its corresponding consequences. There is even theoretical evidence that a sadistic sort of pleasure might be derived from bringing misfortune to others through blame.[76]

The person who never blames is probably not of this world, so good intentions on your part are more than half the battle. If you understand how blame corrodes our daily existence, if you appreciate why we do it nonetheless, and if you truly want to change how you approach adversity, you can indeed make a difference. Individual actions do influence the world (sometimes in a manner far removed in time and space). But our collective actions can achieve wholesale paradigm shifts. So, what follows are some steps we can take to reduce blame.

1. Detach Emotion from Observation

Disappointments, failures, frustrations, set-backs, all take an emotional toll. That emotional pain of something gone wrong can easily morph into a sense of victimization.

If your marriage doesn't provide the sense of adventure you hoped, you might feel deprived. Allowing yourself to feel a victim sets the stage for blaming your spouse for not tuning into, and responding to, your needs.

If you fail to make the football team at high school you will likely feel disappointed. Allowing yourself to feel victimized sets the stage for blaming the coach (who doesn't recognize your talents), your parents (who made you spend too much time on academic study and household chores), and the guy who beat you out for the position (who must have brown-nosed his way into the spot).

If you're a marketing manager and your newest product line has bombed in its three test markets, you're definitely going to be frustrated, and perhaps worried about your job security. Feeling victimized sets the stage for blaming those who designed the product, those who conducted the initial market surveys, those who implemented the test markets, and anyone else who could have influenced the outcome.

Whenever the outcome differs from what we hoped, we are likely to feel wounded, and we may lash-out in an act of self-preservation, retribution, or judgment. But remember: blame never solves the problem. Instead, our first step must be to separate what we feel (our emotional reaction) from what went wrong (our observation of the situation). It's okay to feel like the world has let you down, but recognize the emotion for what it is – a trick of the psyche designed to reduce cognitive dissonance and preserve your self image. When the crisis occurs, if you can retain your composure long enough to acknowledge what you're feeling, and separate that wound from an analytical observation of what went wrong, you will have taken a successful first step.

As I was nearing completion of the first edition of this book, a classic episode of misfortune and blame began to unfold in the Gulf of Mexico. An explosion and fire broke out on an enormous, floating, oil drilling platform - The Deepwater Horizon. Just as nobody expected the World Trade Center towers to collapse after the terrorist jet attacks (everyone was focused on the fire, not the structural integrity of the building), nobody expected the Deepwater Horizon to sink from its fire. But it did. As it sank, the pipe at the well head broke causing the full flow of the oil well to pour directly into the sea. For weeks British Petroleum (BP) tried in vain to figure out how to stem the oil flow. Meanwhile, the environmental disaster grew larger every day. As the first days turned to weeks, pictures of oil-soaked pelicans, plus underwater video of the gushing oil, began dominating the news. Public outrage reached a fever pitch. Gulf coast residents, the nation as a whole, and possibly the entire world all felt violated by this ecological calamity. Predictably, this emotion quickly transformed into intense blame. BP was portrayed as a demon of corporate greed and environmental neglect. The Obama Administration was blamed for not doing something to stop the problem. Both were accused of dragging their feet and not having a sense of urgency about the problem.

Sorely lacking in these first few weeks was a collaborative effort among BP, the federal government, and local Gulf Coast officials to unite and subordinate their own emotional reaction to critical assessment of the predicament. In turn, their united leadership could have helped allay the emotional reaction of the media and public. Had the three entities joined together, had they explained honestly that this was a challenge never faced before and that we lacked an immediate solution, and had they demonstrated their collective resolve to bring all possible resources to bear on this problem, they could have lead the public in detaching the sense of victimization, and refocused on the work that lie ahead.

Does that sort of leadership ever happen? In 1940, England faced a spreading calamity that threatened to wash up on its shores and destroy not only the livelihood of coastal residents, but the existence of British sovereignty itself. No, it wasn't an oil spill, but the rapid expansion of the Nazi Empire. Big mistakes had been made that contributed to this threat. A month earlier as Hitler moved against Holland, Belgium, Luxembourg, and France, the Allies had superior numbers of forces in place to defend against the attack. But the German "blitzkrieg" of swift movement and coordinated communications caught the Allied commanders off guard. Rapidly pushed back to the coast near Dunkirk, 338,000 British and French troops narrowly escaped annihilation only through a miraculous evacuation across the channel. On June 17 France sued for peace, which allowed Hitler to shift his focus to Britain. An uproar echoed throughout the country, "Who was to blame for this blunder that now exposed England to potential doom?"

Prime Minister Winston Churchill could easily have blamed the French for bumbled strategic decisions. He could have blamed his own military planners for not anticipating Germany's actions. He could have blamed previous administrations for not preventing the rise of the Nazi machine. Instead, on June 18, 1940 he appeared before the House of Commons and appealed for suspension of blame and a re-directed focus on how to move forward. His speech was perhaps one of the most stirring examples of a leader setting aside blame, laying out the current predicament, and calling for unity in the face of a dark and ominous threat with uncertain outcomes.

After a brief synopsis of how the predicament had evolved, Churchill said,

> *Now I put all this aside. I put it on the shelf, from which the historians, when they have time, will select their documents to tell their stories. We have to think of the future and not of the past. This also applies in a small*

way to our own affairs at home. There are many who would hold an inquest in the House of Commons on the conduct of the Governments--and of Parliaments, for they are in it, too--during the years which led up to this catastrophe. They seek to indict those who were responsible for the guidance of our affairs. This also would be a foolish and pernicious process. There are too many in it. Let each man search his conscience and search his speeches. I frequently search mine. Of this I am quite sure, that if we open a quarrel between the past and the present, we shall find that we have lost the future.

Churchill didn't hold back on what was at risk, nor did he try to paint a rosy picture that everything was under control. Instead, he said,

. . . if we fail, then the whole world, including the United States, including all that we have known and cared for, will sink into the abyss of a new Dark Age made more sinister, and perhaps more protracted, by the lights of perverted science. Let us therefore brace ourselves to our duties, and so bear ourselves that if the British Empire and its Commonwealth last for a thousand years, men will still say, "This was their finest hour."[77]

Such a check on blame by local, national, and industry leadership is what was needed at the onset of the Gulf oil spill. Instead, the federal government quickly distanced itself by declaring this mess was BP's responsibility. Local leaders positioned themselves as victims of both BP and the federal government. Only BP accepted responsibility for the event and its consequences. Nobody took the leadership to unite the country in facing the challenge. Consequently, America ended up with the most active blame game since hurricane Katrina afflicted the same Gulf Coast areas five years earlier.

Who's to Blame?

Deepwater Bingo				
Capitalism	Dinosaurs	Coast Guard	Shrimp Fishermen	Sarah Palin
Edwin Drake	President Obama	Auto Drivers	Trans-Ocean	Valve Producer
Homeland Security	Republicans	**BP**	Democrats	F.E.M.A.
Illegal Immigrants	Haliburton	Shareholders	President Bush	Marine Scientists
Whaling Industry	Environmentalists	Saudi Arabia	Jed Clampett	Osama Bin Laden

Yes, the oil leak created a horrible environmental situation. Yes, something needed to be done ASAP. Yes, watching pelicans suffocate in oil was heart-wrenching. But pointing fingers was not going to stop the flow of oil any sooner. In fact, blame usually impedes the collective effort needed to deal with systemic problems.

So, when something turns out poorly, the first step must be - stay cool. You can feel like blaming without acting on it. You may feel horribly victimized by the event. Your psyche may cry out to be soothed. But you also have a problem to be solved. And you will likely need an open mind to get to the root of the problem.

This is not easy. Not only will you struggle with your own internal emotions, but you will likely be accused by others as "not having a sense of urgency." Your attempts to remain collected will be viewed by those already blaming as cavalier, or uncaring, or disconnected. If you are in a position of authority people will expect you to be yelling, flailing your arms, and ranting about "whose butt to kick." Don't do it. Real leadership requires you to detach emotion from your observation and assessment of the situation.

2. Assess your own personal responsibility for the problem

If you've successfully separated your emotional reaction from the objective reality of the problem, the next step should be to consider how your own personal responsibility played into the problem scenario. Your role might be seemingly insignificant. It might be far removed in time or space. But the odds are pretty good that if you're affected by a bad event, you also had some kind of role in its occurrence. Taking time to honestly and candidly consider your role serves multiple purposes. First, as you think about your own influence over the situation, you continue to remove yourself from a faulty and counter-productive blame attribution, and you set the stage for the complex thinking that will lead to a systemic understanding of the problem. Second, you can begin to prepare yourself for the kinds of consequences, if any, that you should expect for your share of accountability in the problem. Oftentimes, offering a good description of your own personal responsibility for an issue and an idea of appropriate consequences can head off blame from other stakeholders in the issue.

From the first days of the Gulf oil leak, BP alone declared its responsibility for the problem, and its commitment to make things right. Nearly every other voice jumped on this opportunity to deflect any of their own personal responsibility for this mess. BP would be the scapegoat. The one notable exception was Admiral Thad Allen of the U.S. Coast Guard who was appointed incident commander by the federal government. During the months of BP's attempts to control the escaping oil, he maintained focus on what was being done, and avoided accusations of blame. Perhaps he had thought about how the firefighting tactics after the rig explosion may have actually caused the platform to sink, which, in turn, caused the well pipe to break.

Average Americans sitting at home watching the scenario play out on television could have considered how their own actions and behaviors contributed to the problem. If I drive a 15 mile per gallon Hummer (or a 30 mile per gallon Toyota for that matter) I am the reason we are drilling for oil offshore. There may not be many workable alternatives for me in the short term, other than driving, but my driving is why we're drilling. And without the drilling we wouldn't have the oil spill. So before I go throwing blame, perhaps I need to ask myself: "Am I willing to live with the consequences that derive from my lifestyle?" If so, then I can't really blame someone when they happen. If not, then I need to be making decisions and taking actions to change the status quo.

The President could have called a cabinet meeting and assigned each member to determine the ways in which government actions and policies contributed to this situation. There are certainly many. Armed with that information it would be difficult (in good conscience) to cast blame towards BP. What if, instead of deflecting blame to BP, the White House had stepped forward, and set an example by offering up the following assessment?

> *Deepwater drilling is a relatively new venture for America, and we still have much to learn. Maybe we missed some kind of safety inspection. Maybe we were premature in issuing these permits until we better understood all the potential consequences. Maybe we should have spent the resources for a more robust spill response system. Maybe we should be pursuing alternative energy more aggressively. These are all fair questions to ask, and we will investigate all of these concerns thoroughly. First, however, we are going to focus our efforts on working with BP to figure out how to stem the flow of oil. Then, we are going to focus on damage control. We need to capture as much oil as possible before making landfall, clean up oil that does wash ashore, and conduct any remediation required to restore the environmental impacts. When those priorities are under control we will establish an independent commission, much as was done after 9-11, to learn what we could have done differently and help us plan for the future. In the meantime, I encourage you all to consider how our own lifestyles play into these types of situations,*

what risks we are willing to assume for the choices we make, and how we should best go forward. Your elected representatives need to hear from you so that our future policy-making truly reflects national intent.

Some may think that this admission of contributory responsibility would not have played well politically. Yet public relations and communications experts often suggest that sincere self-reflection plays well with the public, and actually engenders respect. More importantly, if directives within the administration supported this type of public statement, then real progress could be achieved in analyzing the problem to guide future oil-drilling policy. Blame, on the other hand, means every agency and bureau is going to be scrambling to develop its own CYA position.

Gulf Coast elected officials who regularly walk the beaches and look out upon the drilling platforms at sea could ask themselves why they didn't anticipate this possibility. Why hadn't they pressed for construction of sand berms out beyond the marsh habitat? Why hadn't they developed a more serious spill response system that was coordinated with the federal government and oil industry? It's tough to blame someone else when you see what you could have done differently. Coastal officials could also have stepped up with acceptance of contributory responsibility and issued their own statement.

Five years ago we residents of the Gulf Coast struggled through the impact and aftermath of a devastating hurricane. Life is not the same for many, but we have learned that we are survivors. Perhaps because we've focused so intently on steps to avoid this same kind of natural calamity, we have taken our eye off the other risks that can come from the sea. Nobody expected the disaster we are now faced with, so we have not allocated our limited community resources to prevention. But face it now, we must. Consequently, we are joining together the resources of our communities, the Gulf Coast states, the federal government, and the oil industry to solve this problem. We are all in this together. The challenge we

> *face is new to the oil industry, so we seek your patience and your resolve in helping us work through this.*

3. Solve the Problem, not the Symptom

If you've successfully gotten through the first two steps, then you are now prepared to dive into the real work of resolving the issue that caused the pain in the first place. You are no longer asking, "Who's to blame?" but now asking, "What went wrong?"

Problem solving is a broad and complex discipline of its own with a wide array of concepts, strategies, and techniques. Structured approaches to problem solving seem to have been adopted more commonly in the workplace than in either personal relationships or in social-political policy. Response to problems in personal relationships tends to be more reactive and spontaneous, perhaps due to the informality and intimacy of the situation. In the socio-political arena the isolation of agencies and bureaus involved, as well as the adversarial nature of our multi-party political system, hinders a productive response to problems. But even most business and non-profit organizations poorly understand, and minimally practice, structured problem solving. Why is it not more common? Real problem solving is messy business. As we gain an appreciation for the interconnectedness of systems the supply of quick and easy solutions disappears. Part of the appeal of blame is its offer of simplicity. Neat, tidy, black & white solutions are attractive.

But if we're to overcome blame, we need to be prepared to get our hands dirty and get at the real solutions to problems. Most problem solving strategies involve a multi-step process that begins with assessing the scope of the problem and gathering what information or data is known about the problem. The process proceeds into identification of all the known or potential contributory causes of the problem, then prioritizing those causes. Usually multiple solution alternatives are considered and weighed according to predetermined criteria. The best solutions are implemented and then their impact on the problem measured to determine whether the problem has been reduced to a satisfactory level.

The one step of any structured problem-solving process that is most effective in reducing blame is comprehensive root-cause analysis. As systems thinking pioneer Jay Forrester pointed out, we tend to look too close to the symptom for our problem's cause and end up placing blame on a coincident occurrence instead of the real source of the problem. If we can begin to identify all the contributing factors to a problem, then the fallacy of blaming someone becomes much more apparent.

One tool that has gained widespread acceptance and demonstrated great results in assessing contributory causes is the Cause & Effect Diagram. Developed in the 1960s in Japan's Kawasaki shipyards by Kaoru Ishikawa, the tool eventually became a linchpin of quality improvement efforts worldwide. While Ishikawa's original Cause & Effect Diagram used four main branches (Methods, Manpower, Materials, and Machinery) to analyze manufacturing quality problems, today's problem solvers employ various types of tree diagrams or "mind maps," and use the concept to uncover root causes for almost any kind of problem. In any case, just as a map of a watershed basin shows how all the little streams converge into the main river that empties into a large body of water, a Cause & Effect Diagram shows how all the little components to a problem feed into various branches that ultimately empty into the main problem. The technique involves starting with a clear statement of the problem, then exploring back "upstream" to discover all of the sources that feed into the problem.

Continuing with our Deepwater Horizon incident, we would begin by defining the ultimate problem statement: in this case, crude oil polluting the shoreline of the Gulf Coast. At least three main flows feed into this problem: *(a)* the breach of the well, *(b)* demand for oil that creates the need to drill in the first place, and *(c)* response to the leak.

94   Who's to Blame

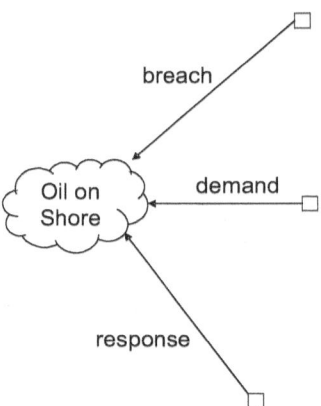

At least three major factors contributed to the actual breach of the well. First, the decision to drill in deepwater means you are working from a floating platform instead of fixed, you have a mile-long, rigid pipe through which the oil must flow, and the well head is in extremely inhospitable conditions 5000 feet below the surface. Ironically, much of the reason for deepwater drilling was to allay the environmental concerns of having drill operations closer in to shore.

Second, the well head valve malfunctioned. This allowed methane gas to the surface, contributing to the explosion. It also failed to shut off when the rig sank and the pipe ruptured. The valve failure may have been caused by a manufacturing defect – perhaps something as simple as a faulty spring or bushing. In addition, the malfunctioning valve might have been caught ahead of time with better maintenance or safety inspection.

Third, the platform, which was not supposed to sink, did. It's possible there was a design, engineering, or construction flaw. There is also speculation that the heavy amount of water used in battling the post-explosion fire actually caused the rig to sink.

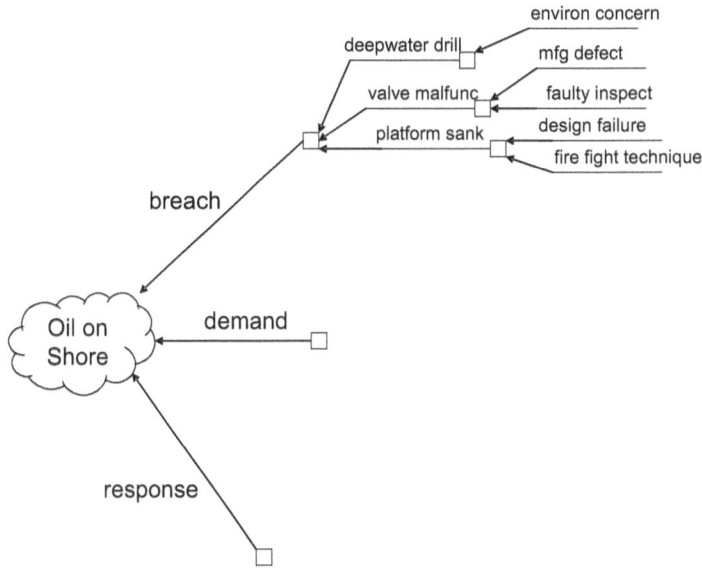

A number of factors drive the demand for oil that necessitated drilling offshore in the first place. A large amount of our crude oil production goes into transportation fuels for automobiles, trucks, airplanes, and so on. But significant amounts of petroleum go into consumer products ranging from insecticides to facial crèmes. In addition, paving asphalt, industrial lubricants, and an assortment of other industrial products rely on oil. Another factor in our current demand is the lack of a progressive energy policy. Our access to inexpensive oil has slowed us from research and development on alternative energy sources.

Looking specifically at transportation fuels, our high demand is driven by our dependence on personal vehicles. This, in turn is driven by the lack of attractive mass transit options, as well as by personal preference for the independence of personal vehicles. High transportation demand is also affected by the fuel efficiency of our transportation fleet. And it is affected by the fact that internal combustion power is an old technology that could be transplanted by more efficient forms (like fuel cells) if we had the social will to make the leap.

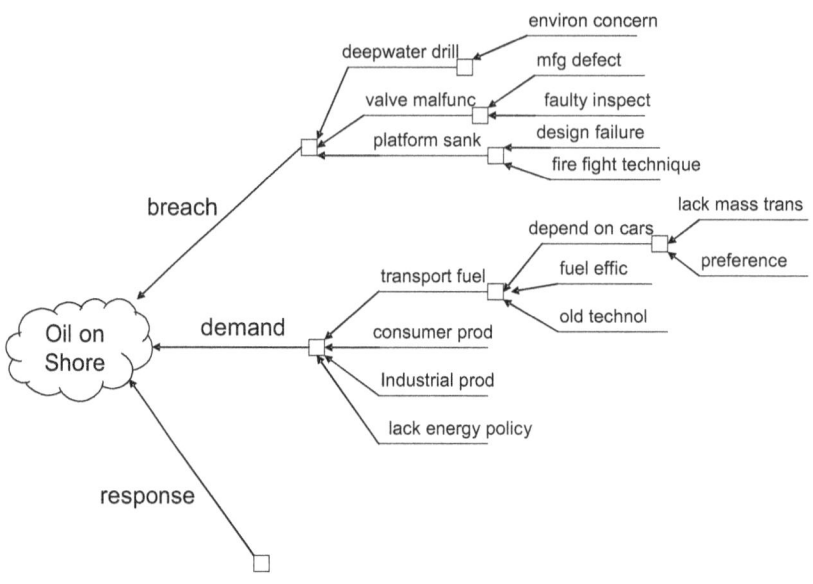

Finally, oil might not have reached the shore if we had responded better to the incident. A highly developed, well-planned, and strongly-funded oil spill response system would likely have helped minimize the amount of oil to reach shore. But nobody really anticipated this disaster – we were operating in virgin territory. And if you don't anticipate something, why would you prepare for it? As a society we have many needs all clamoring for limited resources. In the process of local and national prioritization (of which we all participate by our vote) we collectively did not choose to allocate resources to such an obscure possibility.

Sensitive marshland ecosystems might have been protected if we had paid attention to their exposure to this kind of threat. Over time, environmentally appropriate berms and barrier islands could have been constructed to absorb oil slicks before they penetrated the marshes.

Better response would also have been possible with better coordination of efforts among governmental entities, the oil industry, and foreign aid resources. However, questions of authority, SNAFUs in execution, and unfortunately, political considerations, all impeded the optimization of response performance.

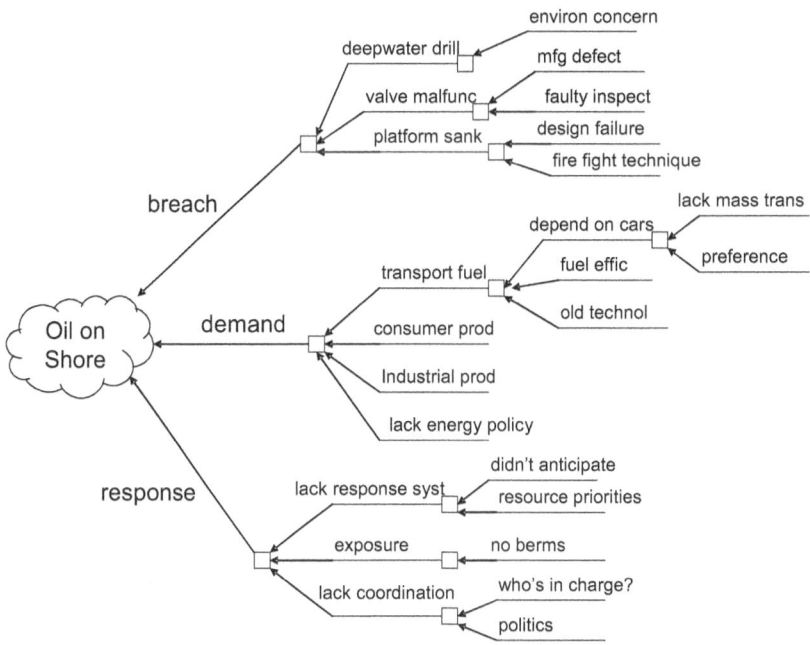

When you break a problem like this down to its many varied root causes, you begin to see that assigning blame is naive at best, and totally dysfunctional at its worst. All of these root causes contributed to oil washing up on the Gulf shores, and millions of people have some degree of personal responsibility for one or more of these root causes. Remove any one, and the problem might not have occurred. But put them all together and you get a systemic result. It's also important to recognize that if we don't resolve the majority of these root causes, a similar type of problem has some statistical probability of occurring again.

Developing a Cause & Effect Diagram to identify the sources of a problem takes time and patience. But it is a great way to move away from the futile practice of laying blame for a problem, and begin moving toward real causes.

4. Create a climate in which blame withers instead of thrives

In every organization the culture tends to mimic the traits of its leadership. If leadership exudes passion about the organizational purpose, employees tend to be focused. If leadership is ostentatious and narcissistic, employees tend to value titles and position over achievement. If leadership obsesses about customer service, employees tend to provide good customer service. If leadership doesn't play by the rules, neither do employees. After 35 years of studying organizational climates I'm still amazed how many leaders believe that they can issue proclamations for their organizations, but somehow remain personally exempt from living by those same proclamations. It never works.

The culture of blame in an organization is no exception. If leadership has a profound understanding of the interconnectedness of events; the distinctions among blame, accountability, and personal responsibility; and the costs of a blaming culture; then, instances of blame are dramatically reduced. Conversely, if leadership continually assigns blame for bad events, that dysfunction will carry throughout the workforce. So, if you are part of the leadership of your organization, reducing blame begins with you. If you don't set the personal example, no amount of organizational development activities, programs, or interventions will accomplish anything. If you talk about finding "whose butt to kick" you can be assured that your followers will look to kick butts instead of solving problems. If you say this problem is someone else's responsibility, your followers will get the message. The good news is: if you do set the example, transforming your organizational culture is very do-able.

As a first step, educate everyone. Employees and managers all need to clearly understand the negative effects blame has on your organization's ability to accomplish its mission. They need to understand that every outcome of the organization results from inter-woven systemic efforts – not the bravado or incompetence of one person. (The successes and failures of the organization are truly collaborative events.) And your workforce needs to understand structured problem solving – especially root cause analysis – if they are to make real headway at resolving the obstacles to success. In some cases providing employees with an assessment tool to determine personal problem-solving styles can help raise self awareness and openness to training about blame.

Once everyone knows about blame, examine the sources and impacts of situational variables within your organization. For example, one situational variable that plagues many organizations is the segregation of various departments and the resultant "we-they" perspective that arises. The tendency to attribute fault to those who are somehow different fans blame. So if departments have strong internal identity, and view other departments as a different "breed," the stage is set for blame attributions. Worse, if departments compete for organizational resources, or even for the attention of leadership, the competition will drive accusations when things go wrong.

Another step leadership can take to create a culture where blame withers is to continuously emphasize organizational goals, ensure that organizational efforts are aligned to those ends, and reinforce how everyone in the organization is in the same boat related to those goals. When people clearly understand their collective objective, and when they know that they all sink or swim together, cultural tolerance for finger-pointing dramatically diminishes.

Finally, in the words of the late W. Edwards Deming, leaders need to "drive out fear" from their organizations. Instead of scapegoating people for events gone wrong, leadership needs to establish a structure of positive accountability versus punitive discipline. Hold people accountable for their thought processes and specific actions as opposed to systemic outcomes. Moreover, to the extent possible, develop predetermined consequences for unacceptable behaviors, and create rational and appropriate corrective measures versus punishment or retribution. Part of this strategy should include securing the involvement of a high quality Employee Assistance Program (EAP) that has the capability to assist in the resolution of blame incidents.

If you are not part of leadership, then reducing blame in your organizational culture becomes much more difficult. But remember: our actions do influence others, and efforts may have consequences far removed in time and space. So start small. By changing your own blaming behaviors, and by speaking up when you hear others blaming someone, you can begin to have a local impact. Perhaps you can even solicit the commitment of your own work team. If you can reduce blame in your immediate environment the quality of your work life may see substantial improvement.

*****

What about reducing blame in the family organization? To reduce the climate of blame within your family environment you can use many of the same ideas. While practices and procedures are much less formalized in a family environment compared to an organizational setting, cultural routines and norms develop nonetheless. Reducing blame within the traditional family must start with parenting. Despite rebellious streaks to the contrary, children do learn, adopt, and emulate their parents' practices. (In families with adult children, the leadership role can become more dispersed as can the blame-reduction initiative.) As in organizational environments, knowledge of blame and its consequences is the place to start. Whether accomplished through family discussions, structured learning, or working with a family counselor, all family members must understand how blame works if you hope to reduce its presence. Next, as in organizational analysis, consider what kinds of situational variables may influence blaming tendencies in the family and correct them where possible. And finally, make sure to base accountability on natural and logical consequences. Kids don't need punishment, but they do need boundaries. Also, just as organizations benefit from contracting with a strong EAP provider, families can benefit from professional help in resolving blame.

The Smiths were a middle class family with two teenage daughters. Relationships around home were frequently contentious. The parents often blamed each other for small things (failure to pay the utility bill on time, bathrooms not clean when in-laws stopped over, checking account dropping below minimum balance, etc.) They also tended to blame each other when either of the daughters got into trouble (poor grades, truancy, failure to pass driver's exam, etc.) As might be expected, the daughters tended to blame the parents for many of their own frustrations (loss of use of car after speeding ticket, missing friend's birthday party due to being grounded, being "dumped" by boyfriend, not having the money to attend a concert, etc.). On the verge of a separation, the parents chose to seek counseling and happened upon a very good counselor (Nancy). Nancy began to explore the degree of blame between the couple, and then among the entire family. She was able to show the parents the link between blame and victimization, and how blame was really an abdication of their own personal responsibility for outcomes. After about 6 months the parents had made visible impact in reducing their blame of each other, and decided to involve their daughters in the counseling. By the time the youngest daughter had graduated from high school, family relations were substantially better than just 3 years prior. During this transformation Nancy had worked with the family on many issues, but the overriding theme throughout had been on eliminating blame.

Whether in an organizational setting or family environment, blame can be reduced through awareness, a clear strategy, and persistent effort. If we can understand our triggers for blame, we can respond more thoughtfully when those triggers are pulled. If we understand the multiplicity of factors that drive any outcome, we can be more intelligent about looking for causes. And if we truly understand the costs that blaming behaviors inflict, we will be more motivated to seek alternatives. Reducing blame generates major paybacks in all facets of our lives. Eliminating blame is good for you! Now the question is: do you have the willpower to see it through?

8

Responding to Blame

A book on blame would be incomplete without addressing what to do when the unthinkable happens – you're the one being blamed! Therefore, this chapter is dedicated to helping you respond when you're the one in the hot seat.

Most people are not well prepared to deal with blame. It's not a subject taught in our schools (though it should be). Most of the time blame catches us off guard - seeming to strike out of the blue. The impact is usually devastating and demoralizing. And we typically are expected to respond at the moment. It can be pretty tough to be the emotional pillar of strength and the compass of rationality when you're the one under attack. But how you handle being blamed when something goes wrong will affect the consequences you face.

Let's start with the bad news: If you're the one being blamed, you're definitely in a hole. The prospects for a good outcome are probably similar to the football team down 21 points at the beginning of the fourth quarter. A happy outcome is possible, but superb execution and a good deal of luck will be required to overcome the odds stacked against you. What's the good news? The right response can dramatically improve your odds. However, one point must be clarified before we begin. This chapter focuses on undoing blame that occurs in your workplace or personal life, where your objective is to correct overblown accountability, eliminate any moral aspersions, and restore interpersonal relationships. If you are blamed for an event that places you under civil or criminal liability you obviously need a really good attorney (who, hopefully, also understands the psychology of undoing blame).

Undoing blame is critically important for several reasons. First, blame imprisons you. Once blamed for something you become saddled with a reputation that automatically makes you a higher-priority suspect for culpability in future problems. Inaction on your part, or acceptance of unwarranted blame, validates the blamer, enables his sense of victimization, and can feed the voracity of the accusation. Second, if blamed for something at work, your motivation and work performance are likely to suffer. This, in turn, can reinforce the perception that you really are to blame for the initial problem. Third, if the event for which you are being blamed is serious enough, the blame can be hazardous to your mental and physical health. There are plenty of examples in which the strain of dealing with unjust accusations has led to interference with other relationships, depression, illness, escapist addictions, even suicide.

If you hope to undo blame in workplace or personal scenarios you must act promptly and assertively. Delays in responding cement the perception of your fault. Time is on the blamer's side. The longer the accusation stands, the more everyone involved gradually moves on to other matters and accepts the accusation at face value.[78] And a weak or timid response encourages more aggression by the accuser in defending the accusation. (Think of how a snarling dog senses fear or insecurity and emboldens its attack stance.)

Before you respond, a self-check is warranted. What is your level of personal responsibility for the event in question? And, given your own accountability, what consequences would be appropriate? After all, mistakes are human. When Ethel and Myrtle mixed up the shipping labels at Nuts-n-Bolts Company, product was sent to the wrong customers. Having been reliable and loyal employees for three years, perhaps acknowledgement of the mistake and its impact, along with a suggested process to double-check all shipping labels could be appropriate consequences. Proactive acceptance of that level of accountability might have defused the blame, had the problem not already spiraled out of control. But how far should you go? Were your actions reasonable with the information at your disposal? If the blame is out of proportion to your level of accountability for the problem, reassure yourself that you are okay. You know what happened. You know how you contributed to the result. You know what you would change next time. You are not a worthless loser. You are simply an unfortunate scapegoat. You understand how blame works, the irrationality of it, and why people get caught up in blaming others. So it is now time to make your stand.

Don't go it alone if you don't need to. Using a facilitator can be highly effective in developing your game plan and confronting the blamer. The best facilitator will be someone respected by the blamer and knowledgeable about blaming behavior. A good facilitator can provide objective feedback while you develop your response strategy. Then, the facilitator can help break the ice and set a constructive communication stage when you actually sit down to talk to the blamer. If your organization provides an Employee Assistance Program (EAP), that might be a good place to find your facilitator.

Now, build your response ahead of time. You want to go into your confrontation with a clear strategy. Prepare your thoughts around an outline. There are many suggested approaches to conflict resolution available from many sources. And you know your personal situation better than anyone. I've had good results, both personally and in coaching others, with the following six-step approach.

Acknowledge the situation and the "wound."

Remember that blame is less about facts than about feelings. The blamer often feels victimized by the event that occurred. The "wound" may be as simple as embarrassment over the incident. It could be as serious as personal financial loss. The person blaming you might also have been caught in a chain of blame by someone else. If at all possible, find out ahead of time what feelings are driving the blame. Then open your conversation with an acknowledgement. "Fred, I want you to know that I feel bad about what happened yesterday – especially that it caused you to… (whatever the impact)." Being human, the blamer may choose to vent a bit of his feelings at this point. As long as the venting does not turn abusive you can use this opportunity to better understand your blamer's hot buttons. Remember again: this is about feelings. Validate them where you honestly can.

Re-affirm your shared values or goals.

Being the scapegoat for a situation is probably more about a situational variable than about your real contribution to the problem. Most likely your blamer initially zeroed in on you due to circumstantial factors as opposed to truly believing you intended to do him evil. Once you became the scapegoat, the blamer probably began to reinforce his thinking that you were at fault. Re-assuring the blamer that you share the same values, and that you want to achieve the same collaborative goals, may suspend any demonization taking place in his head. "You know I share the values we espouse in this organization, and I definitely want us to be successful in... (reaching whatever goals are involved)."

Review your decision process.

The blamer is likely puzzled over how, or why, you could have done what you did to mess things up so badly (in his eyes). He clearly doesn't understand the perspective from which you acted. So tell him. By simply walking through the decision process or situational factors leading up to your involvement you can open a new level of awareness for the blamer. But be careful. Do not be making excuses or self-justifications for your true level of shared accountability. Just objectively recount how your involvement unfolded. This will help re-focus the blamer away from you and onto the process.

Suggest a fix.

If there was a flaw in your decisions or actions contributing to the problem, this is the place to point it out. "Given... (the information you had at the time) I chose to do... (the offending action). But I can see now that what I should have done was... (better action)."

This reassures the blamer that you actually do "get-it" and are not simply useless, incompetent, malicious, or whatever other negative attribute has been dominating his thinking. Then follow this up with a suggestion to prevent a re-occurrence by anyone in the same situation. That could be improved access to information, a checkpoint to validate the decision before acting, or any other idea to avoid the same problem in the future.

Get commitment on the fix.

If the blamer is still with you at this point, you can complete the shift from blame to process improvement by asking the blamer for his commitment to implementing the suggested fix. The discussion can move to how we go forward. If there are some left-over impacts from the problem that still need cleaning-up, this would also be a good time to discuss how to resolve them. Understand that at this stage you may need to accept some reasonable and appropriate consequences for whatever accountability you shared in the problem, but you should be on your way to extinguishing the blame.

Ask for input on restoring relationships.

Finally, assuming you truly want to restore yourself to full respect in the eyes of the blamer, ask for his input. "You know, I understand that this incident has put me on the black list with some of my team members, and it may have damaged my relationship with you. Do you have any suggestions for how I can mend those bridges? It's hard to be completely effective if people mistrust you." Assuming for a moment that your blamer is also truly interested in the welfare of your organization, this type of request will go a long way toward eliminating any lingering dissonance the blamer might have about letting go of blame.

Sometimes football teams overcome a big deficit in the fourth quarter to win the game. And sometimes a scapegoat can free itself from the crushing burden of blame. One can only try. This six step approach is probably your best bet when responding to blame.

Afterword

Congratulations! Having read this far, you've embarked on a journey of transformation that will likely continue for the rest of your life. Once you see blame for what it is - revealed without all of its self-justifications - then it becomes difficult to revert back to old ways of thinking. Every time you feel victimized by some event or personal behavior, a little part of you deep inside will begin to question your instinctive desire to blame someone. That's not surprising if you think about it. You now know quite a bit about blame. You've seen examples of its destructive wake. You've learned about blame's cultural roots, some of the psychology behind it, and the situational variables that trigger it. You've explored how the systemic nature of events renders blame irrational. You've seen how blame differs from logical consequences, and also from personal responsibility. And, you've acquired some tactics for reducing blame.

Now the question becomes: what will you do with this knowledge? If you are someone with a highly external locus of control, maybe you will simply use it to help you cope when someone culls you out as the culprit for a mishap. If you feel a bit more like controlling your destiny, you may choose to push back against this blame. Or maybe, if you have a strong internal locus of control, you will decide to take this knowledge and launch a crusade to change the world around you.

Most of us want to extricate ourselves when we become the scapegoat for some bad thing that has happened. But the real "world-changing" stuff comes when we decide to alter our own approach to blame, and even more so when we begin to set an example for others to follow. So, ask yourself right now, "Am I willing and ready to give it up?"

Blame does serve some emotional purposes. It helps us reduce cognitive dissonance when an event conflicts with our internal self image. It helps us avoid negative consequences for problems in which we subconsciously know we might have contributed to the outcome. And, if we have a personal score to settle with someone, or even if our sadistic inclinations simply run high, we might actually get a kick out of blame.

In some ways, giving up on blame is like quitting an addiction. Besides the "high" we might experience from its use (or abuse), the habit is deeply ingrained into the innermost regions of our psyche. Cessation may leave you feeling awkward, until you assimilate replacement behaviors – like contemplating systemic root causes. And, you might be tempted to "fall off the wagon" from time to time and revert to blaming behaviors.

But like most addictions, blame is also terribly dysfunctional – to you, and to those around you. If others look up to you (whether in a family setting, a work place, or in society) your example of blame sets the tone for others to follow, and could potentially lead to that entity's ultimate demise. And don't forget the old maxim, "everything you do will come back to you," because the person you blame today may have an even greater opportunity to get even in the future.

The promise, looking forward, is that you can begin to have an impact in your home and your workplace almost immediately. Start anywhere. If you drop an egg on the kitchen floor (seemingly, because the carton was grossly off-balance), pause and take note that reality (I dropped an egg) is dissonant from your self image (I'm totally coordinated). Ask yourself how you might have contributed to this outcome. (Maybe I'm not using my normally-coordinated grip when I grab the egg carton.) Then, if you want your spouse to help prevent the problem in the future, you can still show how you just dropped an egg, and ask for his/her help by keeping the carton balanced. The payoff to you will be a better relationship. It's worth noting here that certified family counselors are often knowledgeable about the psychological aspects of blame. So, if you are tackling serious blame issues within your family, a good counselor can be a tremendous ally.

If you're a leader in your organization, start with your key staff. Explain how blame impedes organizational performance, and that you'd like to begin a "search and destroy" mission to identify where blame tends to occur, and to substitute systemic thinking or root cause analysis. I think you'll find your staff surprisingly receptive to the idea. Through the years I have worked with many organizations in identifying the internal dynamics that promote blame, then changing those dynamics to create positive environments. In every case, when leadership led the charge, those organizations were able to build cultures in which the costs of blame were gradually displaced with engagement and entrepreneurial spirit.

If you're working at a more grass-roots level and want to begin to change your workplace, don't go it alone. Get a few others on board. Giving up smoking, or losing 15 pounds, is a lot more successful if you build a supportive alliance of collaborators with the same goal. Likewise, transforming a culture of blame in your work team will be easier (and you'll stay more on track) if you solicit a group commitment to that objective. If your organization participates in an EAP (Employee Assistance Program) you may find additional resources and support there to get your effort underway.

Changing the use of blame in our larger societal context is a tougher challenge. Politics employs blame as a strategic tool. The belief is, that by making my opponent look bad, I look better. Mud-slinging campaigns are the norm today. Hopefully, as a voter who now understands blame a bit better, you can incorporate that knowledge in choosing your candidate. If we all reject candidates who campaign on blame, we may end up with a better caliber of political leaders.

Then, there is the issue of blame in the media. As pointed out in the opening paragraph of Chapter 1, blame dominates our news media. The viability of media outlets depends heavily on ratings, which depend on providing audiences what they want. To the extent that you begin to want more than a superficial witch hunt on the cause of current events, let your media outlets know. If you'd prefer to see thoughtful, in-depth analysis of issues, you need to speak up. Today there is an enormous realm of opportunity to make your voice heard. You can respond directly to online news by posting your own comments. Most media outlets also have

Facebook pages where you can post comments. Many radio and television station managers actively solicit e-mail response to their programming. Local newspapers encourage letters to the editor. If you want more than blame… tell them!

At times, life along the societal fault line can be disheartening. The prospect of reducing blame can seem overwhelming. But one lesson I've learned, over and over again, is that individual actions can make a difference. The impact may be far removed in time and space from the action. But, sooner or later, your efforts to curtail blame yield dividends to someone. Speak up when you see blame. Point out contributing factors when you are observing from the sideline. Respond intelligently when you are unfairly targeted. Your leadership and your voice can begin the transformation.

Living along society's fault line doesn't need to be so treacherous if we all stop looking for who's to blame.

*****

Note from the author:

Potential readers considering the purchase of this book rely upon comments and reviews from people like you who've already read it. I'd greatly appreciate your taking a few minutes and posting an honest review on the book's Amazon page. Your thoughts are truly valuable to the person wondering if this book is right for them.

Also, I enjoy hearing directly from my readers. Feel free to contact me through my website:
                    www.DanLinssen.com

There, you can also sign up for my quarterly newsletter, which contains insightful tidbits on a variety of literary subjects, humorous anecdotes, and updates on my current projects. You will also receive a free copy of my short story *Scout Camp*, a fun portrait of two young boys in the 1950s as they maneuver their way through their first week-long adventure at Boy Scout camp.

Appendix

Blame in the Workplace

Many people invest the majority of their waking hours in the workplace. These workplaces might be enormous and complex global corporate enterprises. Sometimes they are as intimate and simple as a small retail shop. Common to them all is the presence of blame and the specific impacts blame carries on the accomplishment of organizational purpose. For that reason, this appendix explores the nature of blame and its associated impacts in the workplace.

Most organizations, in business, education, healthcare, government, and the non-profit sector, seriously constrain their ultimate performance by passively accepting (perhaps even unwittingly promoting) blaming behaviors, which become imbedded into the organizational culture. In our organizational environments, "results" reign paramount. The search for whom to blame when bad things happen seems natural. And once the culprit is found, we then either apply appropriate disciplinary actions, or cull the offending member from the herd.

This happens thousands of times every day throughout the workplace. It happens to CEOs when earnings per share don't measure up to stock market expectations. And it happens to a frontline production employee when a quality defect passes unnoticed to the customer. In business workplaces, salespersons are blamed for not making their quota, maintenance technicians are blamed for mechanical breakdowns that halt production, warehouse personnel are blamed for damaged inventory, and cost analysts are blamed for pricing assumptions that don't turn out as planned. In education, teachers are blamed for low standardized test scores, site administrators are blamed for bad hiring decisions, coaches are blamed for losing seasons, and superintendents are blamed for budget overruns. In healthcare, physicians are blamed for procedures that don't yield intended outcomes, diagnostic technicians are blamed for erroneous test results, administrators are blamed for failing accreditation standards, and nurses are blamed for not responding to all patient needs quickly enough. In government agencies, employees are blamed for not adhering to tightly defined policies, and managers are blamed for complaints from the public sectors served.

This all seems a perfectly normal part of responding to the crises that occur every day in every organization. After all, people "mess-up," so they must be held accountable, right? There is an enormous desire among leaders to know "who was at fault" when a problem occurs. The process of blaming someone and dispensing an appropriate punishment (i.e. disciplinary action) seems to be the right thing to do. How else does one maintain order in an enterprise where the next crisis is right around the corner? But finding the culprit and administering disciplinary action may not be the solution it appears. And the yellow caution flags have been waving for a long time.

A half-century ago in the January/February 1964 issue of Harvard Business Review, professor Charles Gragg challenged business leaders of the era with a thought-provoking piece entitled, "Whose Fault Was It?" In the article, Gragg argued that finding fault is a futile and misdirected effort. In Gragg's words, "'Whose fault was it?' is a profoundly complicated question, one that is essentially unanswerable, and one that cannot be asked safely. It is a profoundly disturbing question that at the very least produces waste and that more commonly produces tragedy."[79] Unfortunately, Gragg's seminal observations are not a critical component of management curricula at our universities.

Twenty years later W. Edwards Deming, who is credited with guiding Japan's rise to industrial power in the 1970s, tried to get legions of leaders to understand that blame was a futile expenditure of emotion. Deming's rationale was that problems are caused by the system and not by individual people. He confronted leaders to "drive out fear" from their organizations so people could focus on doing their jobs instead of worrying about being blamed for something that might go wrong.[80]

Despite generations of warnings about the consequences of blame, today blame remains, as much as ever, a cancer slowly destroying the ability of our organizations to function effectively. To better understand how blame works in an organizational setting let's take a more in-depth look at the story of one business.

Acme Plastics

Acme Plastics (fictitious name, but based on a real scenario) is a medium-sized plastics company. Several years ago the company purchased a site in a small southern town and built a production plant producing components for automotive interiors. A combination of virgin plastic and recycled plastic is injected into large production presses to make the parts, so skilled labor is critical. However, a major manufacturer who was previously located there had moved "off-shore," so a large skilled labor force was available in the community and eager to go to work. Since construction of this plant the automotive segment of Acme's business has grown rapidly. One customer (Big Auto - a major auto producer) now purchases 55 percent of total plant output. So far, Acme's plant has managed to increase their capacity to meet these demands. But, because Big Auto requires Just-In-Time (JIT) delivery on the parts, trying to meet their schedule with no shortages has been a challenge for the new team at Acme. (See business diagram.)

116   *Who's to Blame*

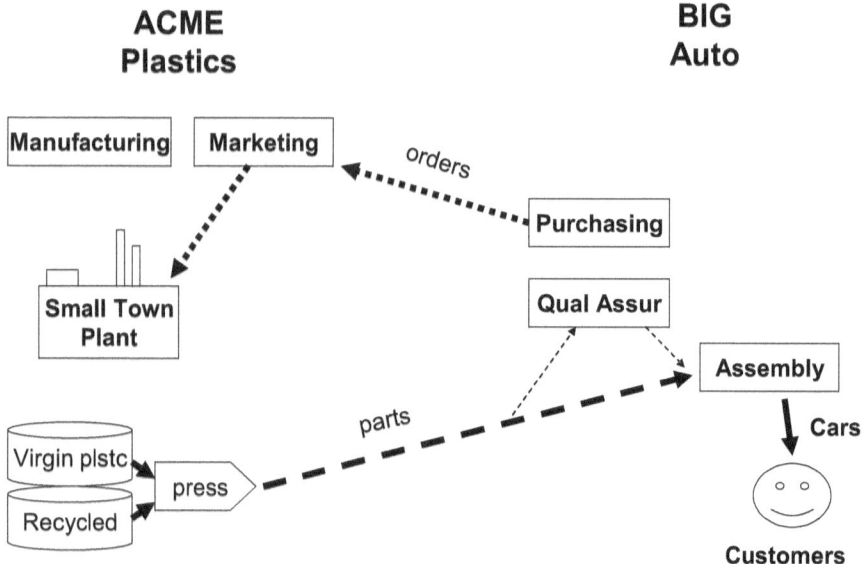

As with many rapid-growth operations, this Acme plant experienced a number of growing pains. Managers focused more on hiring and training new employees, sourcing adequate production materials, and expanding plant capacity than on fine-tuning policies and procedures. Crises seemed to arise daily, but somehow the plant team always worked through them. In one particular incident six months earlier, a serious mechanical breakdown in one of the high-volume presses caused Acme to "short" an order to Big Auto. Due to Acme's just-in-time inventory arrangement with the customer, this shortage resulted in a full-day stoppage in one of Big Auto's assembly lines. Big Auto's purchasing department took a lot of heat from senior management for not having a reliable parts source. So, needless to say, the Big Auto purchasing group is not very happy with Acme at the moment. In response, Acme plant management has encouraged production teams to take the initiative on developing ideas that will speed production, expand capacity, or find cost reductions that could be passed along to the customer as lower pricing.

Most Acme products use a combination of virgin and recycled plastic. With their own plastics recycling facility in a nearby town, sourcing of recycled material has not been a problem. However, due to fluctuations in oil markets, the delivery of virgin plastic resin has been unpredictable – sometimes constraining production volume. Two weeks ago one of the production teams experimented with their process and discovered that they could reduce the percentage of virgin plastic resin from 40% to 20% with no apparent impact on the quality of the finished product. The team solicited help from a tech in their quality assurance department and ran a number of tests on product appearance and durability and could find no difference. Given the high need for virgin plastic in another product line, and the current limited supply, this team decided to cut the percentage of virgin plastic in their current part.

What they didn't know was that the ratio of virgin-to-recycled plastic had been specified by Big Auto in their product purchase order. That particular requirement was not a major part of the specification, and it was buried in the fine print of the order. But it was there. Now, after running the part with the new formulation for two weeks, shipping the product to the customer, and having those parts installed in new automobiles, someone in Big Auto's quality assurance department discovered the off-spec plastic formulation while conducting a random audit.

It didn't take long before Big Auto's purchasing manager was on the phone to Acme's vice president of marketing. The purchasing manager was livid. He would need to present this problem to his division executive team to determine if installing the off-spec part for the past couple weeks created any product liability issues. (Nobody likes to run bad news "up the flagpole.") He told Acme's VP of marketing that if he had another alternative he would "pull the plug" on their business right now.

After enduring this savage telephone assault, Acme's marketing VP stormed down the hall into the office of the manufacturing VP and unloaded with both barrels (verbal arsenal and emotional discharge). Caught off guard and on shaky ground, the manufacturing VP had little defense. He subsequently called the plant manager to find out why the heck the plant was arbitrarily changing product specs. Unfortunately, the plant manager had not been informed of the process change, so he appeared to be totally out of control of plant operations. In response, the plant manager hastened out to see the young and inexperienced production team leader, who didn't realize this was a customer spec issue and thought he was doing something good. When he made the decision, the team leader hadn't wanted to bother the plant manager with the details because the plant manager was tied up with purchase negotiations for some new production equipment.

Back at Acme corporate headquarters the marketing VP was lobbying the company president for heads to roll in manufacturing. This was the second major problem the production plant had caused in Acme's relationship with Big Auto, and it jeopardized the entire account. According to the marketing VP, this was just another example proving that the entire manufacturing team didn't take customer satisfaction seriously. After all, the plant had a full copy of the customer purchase order and all specifications therein. Didn't they feel it was important to pay attention to written specifications? At a minimum, the marketing VP wanted the plant manager replaced with someone who understood corporate priorities, and the VP of manufacturing severely chastised for not building a customer-focused culture.

The manufacturing VP responded that the new plant had basically accomplished miracles by ramping production sufficiently to meet the huge volume required by Big Auto. This account wouldn't even be possible if they hadn't managed to find a way to deliver the product demanded. He felt marketing shirked their responsibility by not working with the customer to explain what had happened and why, and by not re-assuring Big Auto of Acme's commitment to meet their needs. And, if a particular specification was so important, why hadn't marketing better communicated the significance of the spec instead of just forwarding a copy of the purchase order to the plant with no follow-up emphasis? The manufacturing VP felt that marketing needed to become a team player, dive into the trenches, and help resolve this issue with the customer instead of just wining and dining prospects to get their business.

Who's to Blame?

Thoughtful people who happen to be at or near ground-zero when a workplace problem explodes usually realize very quickly how their actions contributed to the problem, and they understand what might have been done differently. At the same time, they just as quickly know that many other factors, lying outside their control (or at least their field of vision), contributed to the problem. Moreover, they often know that if the clock were re-wound and the incident re-played, they'd probably take the same series of actions again, at least without some different information at their disposal or different set of situational variables.

Who should take the fall for this problem? The plant manager is clearly responsible for the activities in that plant, so he could be expected to offer himself up in sacrifice for the off-spec production run. If Acme loses Big Auto's business, the consequences to the plant manager might be the loss of his job. If the issue blows over with Big Auto, the plant manager might get by eating some "humble pie" for awhile until some other issue in the company takes center stage. But he's been a capable manager who has held things together in the chaotic growth of a new plant. What good comes from giving him the boot? The production team leader (whose group made the process change and ran parts with more recycled plastic) could also come forward and accept accountability. After all, he actually made the unauthorized change. Given the degree of consternation that occurred at the senior management level, the team leader is probably at greater risk of termination than the plant manager, and would certainly face some kind of disciplinary action – which is always more common at lower levels of the organization. But given the team leader's sense of initiative and desire to be successful, any kind of discipline is likely to dampen his attitude. Perhaps the marketing account manager who took the purchase order from Big Auto should come forward and accept accountability, since he did not adequately communicate the importance of the plastic specification to the production team. Maybe the manufacturing VP or marketing VP is accountable, since neither of them had sufficient procedures in place to prevent the problem in the first place. But no matter who takes the fall for this problem, they all have a sense that the problem was not their fault.

Acme has some real problems that need to be fixed. Obviously an action that jeopardizes the company's largest customer account should never have happened. But confessions are useless. Everyone was doing their best – or so they thought. A confession won't get into the complex, interwoven root causes of this issue, so a similar event could easily happen again. Moreover, blaming someone for the problem will instill resentment and bad attitudes among one or more key players at a time when Acme needs everyone's best contribution. Blame does not solve Acme's problem with Big Auto because the problem wasn't caused by a person.

The Buck Stops Here (with you, that is)

Some organizations try to finesse the issue of blame by espousing some value in their culture that expects employees to step forward and admit guilt for problems as they arise. Such cultural expectations are often couched in the more organizationally palatable lingo of "accepting responsibility." But they really amount to little more than a ritualistic offering-up of oneself as the sacrificial lamb to appease the blame gods. The CEO of one company once told me, "When a problem occurs I expect the responsible person to come forward and say 'I screwed up.' That simple admission relieves a lot of tension and allows us to move on." This sounds innocuous enough. In effect, the supervisor (or manager, or board of directors) is appeased that whoever caused the problem has been identified, and accountability dispensed. The presiding blamer may (but not always) afford some degree of leniency in exchange for the confession, depending upon the severity of the situation, the past history of the offender, the mood of the boss, and other variables. The problem with this practice: it's just an elaborate game – an insincere, ritualistic exercise that must be endured every time something goes wrong. You could think of it as institutionalized blame. Leadership, having assigned blame and received a suitable confession, satisfies itself that the offending employee now understands the error of his ways and commits to do better next time. Meanwhile, the employee (who usually doesn't really believe he is at fault) submits to the expected confession and resultant consequences hoping they will be minor. This practice may indeed relieve some tension and allow everyone to move on (short-term gain) but it is still blame and comes with the same costs.

Organizational Costs of Blame

Blame doesn't solve whatever issues contributed to a workplace problem in the first place. And, more importantly, there are hidden costs which tend to accumulate over time and lead to long-term organizational cancers. Let's consider some of these dysfunctional consequences.

Subversion – spreading a mood of discontent and disrespect

Someone blamed for an organizational problem typically knows they've taken the fall for something with many more contributory factors. This generates resentment and cynicism, and can lead to a contagious lack of faith in, or respect for, organizational leadership. A blamed employee will likely complain about the incident to his co-workers later, around the water cooler, or at happy hour, or on the golf course. He might joke about the tongue-lashing received in the "principal's office" if the punishment was minor, or he may resort to openly berating the boss if the punishment was seen as unjust. And, he will always assert that blame for the problem really lies elsewhere. Co-workers see the drama play out, recognize the inequity in the blame, empathize with the accused victim, fear for their own security, and begin to question the wisdom of their leaders.

Gamesmanship

Because blame lacks a real solution to the problem, a culture of blame sends a strong message throughout the organization that authenticity is not a key corporate value. Employees learn to play the game in which those accused profess contrition for the error of their ways and vow commitment to do better next time. This in turn breeds other forms of gamesmanship which are deemed acceptable, played, and perfected. Eventually, most blaming cultures spawn other forms of inauthentic behaviors such as back-stabbing, credit-grabbing, or brown-nosing – none of which are very beneficial to peak organizational performance.

Playing it Safe

When people are subjected to blame and disciplinary consequences for workplace problems, it doesn't take long for the average employee to recognize the need to play it safe. Don't do anything that could potentially put you in jeopardy of being part and parcel to a mistake. You definitely don't want to be the one bearing accountability. And what could increase the odds of making a mistake more than calculated risk-taking, outside-the-box creativity, or leading an initiative to make something happen? Acme leadership may think assigning blame (and disciplining the team or team leader involved in the off-spec product) will emphasize the importance of paying attention to customer specifications. But they will certainly diminish the willingness of employees to freely invent and try new ideas. The team that changed the production process was looking for a way to prevent raw material shortages throughout the plant, and perhaps to reduce the cost of the product to the customer. Their idea and actions had little personal payoff other than helping Acme grow and be successful. They were not competing for some financial gain awarded to best new idea. So what incentive do they have to continue trying new ideas if there is an inherently high risk of blame for failure? A much safer (and easier) route is to follow directions and do what you're told, rather than explore, invent, and initiate new ideas for progress.

Brain Drain

Acme desperately needs its best and brightest employees to figure out how to continue to grow the business while at the same time maintaining internal control to avoid similar future problems. But in a culture of blame, the best "A-team" intelligent risk-takers are eventually lost to other organizations as they look for environments where they are freer to experiment and appreciated for their talents. What remains are the least creative, least ambitious players who are content to be "yes-men" followers.

We like to think that identifying the culprit and assigning blame solves the problem. In the case of a serious problem we sometimes move to eliminate the problem by terminating the person associated with the problem. But history shows us that our terminated culprit often moves to another organization and enjoys a stellar career. And sooner or later the problem we thought we eliminated re-occurs. In such circumstances the cost of blame may be the loss of a valuable human asset – perhaps even to a key competitor. Such loss of a good contributor can also adversely affect morale among remaining team members.

Blissful Unawareness

Let us make a couple of changes in the Acme story. First let us assume that Acme's culture is characteristically high in blame. Everyone knows that when something goes wrong, someone will pay. Then let us assume that the off-spec product was not discovered by Big Auto's quality assurance department. Instead, two weeks into the production change the plant manager is eating lunch with the team leader (whose team has changed the plastic formulation) and casually finds out about the change. Something in the back of the plant manager's head is uneasy about this news but he's not sure why. Upon returning to his office he looks at the purchase order and discovers the fine-print specification regarding use of recycled plastic. He now realizes that the product going out the door is technically not in spec. He doesn't see a problem with the part as currently produced, but it doesn't meet written customer specifications.

The plant manager may have a strong personal code of ethics and integrity. But the culture of blame will create tremendous disincentive to pass this information up the chain of command. Most likely the plant manager will at least consider simply changing the formulation back to specification and not say anything to his boss. With any luck, the parts will not pose a problem to anyone and all will be good. No sense upsetting the apple cart if all the apples are good (even if some Macintosh are mixed in with the Pippins). And if anything should be discovered, at least he can claim that he took immediate action once the off-spec condition was revealed.

Leaders throughout the world might be shocked to learn of the number of problems hidden below the surface in their organizations, just festering and waiting for the necessary trigger mechanism to explode into major crises. In high-blame cultures the leader primarily hears what he wants to hear. Only when catastrophe strikes is bad news forced upward. Minor mistakes (or those that have not yet fully ripened) are not readily communicated upward. There is always hope that consequences will be minimal or non-existent and blame will be avoided. Many leaders continually operate in this unrealistic limbo of unawareness. Unfortunately, if you were to ask them, most of those same leaders are convinced they are well informed on the status of their organization.

See no Evil, Hear no Evil

Not only are people reluctant to pass problem information up the chain of command in high-blame cultures, but there is even strong incentive to avoid seeing or hearing bad things altogether. Suppose that the Acme quality assurance tech who helped the team test its product formulation changes was in the plant manager's office a week later and came across the purchase order for the product. For a moment he wondered if he should review the purchase order for anything that might raise a red flag on the process change. But the desire to distance himself from any potential problem caused him to decide against even looking at it. If he were to find a conflict in the purchase order, then he could become partly to blame for producing an off-spec problem. If he remains unaware of any potential specification, then he feels he retains his innocence.

CYA

If the Acme plant manager gets blamed for the process error, one possible reaction might be to implement some kind of formal approval process in which any proposed process changes would be screened through a checklist of questions with a written report detailing the findings. For example:

    Does the proposed change comply with all customer product specifications?

    What potential unforeseen product changes could result from this process change?

Blame in the Workplace   125

Does the change require any new materials or equipment not currently in use?

What knowledge, expertise, or information do we need about the use of these materials or equipment?

How will changes to the product be monitored after implementation of the process change?

What impact will the proposed change have on other process variables?

The findings could then be written up and passed to the marketing and quality assurance departments for their approval.

Perhaps such a formalized review process is a good idea and should be implemented, especially if the consequences of a process change could be significant to the company. But it also encumbers both efficiency and flexibility of the operation. Resources (in some cases enormous resources) could end up being diverted from productive activity into defensive activities that don't yield any concrete benefit. When I'm a passenger in a commercial airliner I certainly want the pilot to run through a pre-flight checklist before taking off. But I probably don't want to wait for him to write a formal report on his findings and pass it to the airline operations manager, FAA, and National Transportation Safety Board for approval before take-off.

A culture of blame quickly leads to a culture of CYA - Cover Your... Accountability. Therein, very little action occurs without supporting documentation that protects against being held responsible for unexpected results. Elaborate systems of documentation arise to account for any possible occurrence that can be imagined. And individual efforts end up being supported by memos, notices, requests for authorization, or any other kinds of evidence that the person is not solely accountable for his actions. Government operations are frequently the object of jokes about the degree of bureaucracy – largely because they are highly bureaucratic. However, in a competitive market environment, an organization bogged down in procedure rarely remains viable in the long run. Flexibility and responsiveness tend to be paramount to success. So while excess review and documentation activities can offer individuals some defense against blame, they come at a high cost to the organization. Anyone who has had organizational responsibility for maintaining the documentation for ISO certification, JCHO accreditation, Sarbanes-Oxley compliance, or any other bureaucratic requirement to validate organizational reputation understands the cost of such documentation. Ironically, the piles of documentation usually associated with CYA environments are generally ineffective at shielding against blame. In most organizations an unimaginable realm of potential things can go wrong with any decision made. Anticipating and pre-justifying all of these potential outcomes is virtually impossible. Just when you think you have a good alibi, a new twist in the plot leaves you vulnerable.

Motivational Asphyxia

Perhaps the greatest cost of blaming cultures to organizations of all types is the impact on motivation and morale. Study after study reveals a persistent low level of job satisfaction in the workplace. One recent study indicated job satisfaction at a 22 year low and only 45% of the workforce satisfied with their current job.[81] Another study showed that at any point in time 65% of existing workers are actively looking for a different job.[82] Everyone understands what is meant by Monday morning blues. But we continually fail to connect the dots in changing this environment and finding the secret to truly engaging our employees. Most employees are not highly dissatisfied with the tasks they perform. And most are not highly disillusioned with their compensation. The real issue in job dissatisfaction is the feeling of not being valued. And nothing kills a sense of value more quickly than blame.

Blame destroys self-esteem. The judgmental nature of blame ties a person's involvement with a problem to their worth as a human being. Being blamed is often humiliating, and it's tough to exhibit your best performance when your self-image is below sea-level. Emotional effort directed toward recovery of self-image becomes emotional effort not available for accomplishing the organizational mission. If a sizeable portion of your workforce's emotional energy is being directed to maintaining self esteem instead of moving the organization forward, if intrinsic motivation is low, and if employees are actively seeking outside opportunities, long-term viability faces serious jeopardy.

Retribution

A less frequent, but potentially more catastrophic, consequence of blame can be retribution by the blamed individual. Incidences of workplace shootings involving supervisors or co-workers often relate to the blaming of an individual. Between 1983 and 1993 there were 11 incidents in the U.S. Postal Service in which employees opened fire on their bosses and co-workers. Most of these incidents involved the termination or discipline of an employee. 35 postal employees were killed and another 26 wounded in these incidents.[83] In March of 2010, a recently hired, 51 year-old Ohio State University janitor named Nathaniel Brown, received a letter from his supervisors stating he was being terminated because he was tardy and had problems following instructions. Brown complained to the union that his supervisors were being unfair, but the union wouldn't do anything unless he submitted a written, formal complaint. The next day Brown walked into the maintenance building, shot the two supervisors, then killed himself.[84]

These types of incidents happen far too frequently. More disturbing is the indication they are on the rise. According to studies by the National Safe Workplace Institute in Chicago, the most dramatically increasing type of workplace violence is employer-directed. Until late 1992, data shows an average of one employer-directed homicide per month in the United States. As of 2009 the rate had escalated to an average of five or six monthly.[85]

People who resort to homicide in retaliation for blame are generally distressed to the breaking point and are unconcerned about their own fate. But many individuals, equally enraged by blame, find stealthier ways to get their revenge. As more of our organizational life depends upon technology, viral infections, outright crashes, or loss of critical data become increasing targets of disgruntled employees. Machinery and equipment breakdowns, arson, chemical leaks, contamination, theft, transfer of proprietary information, libel, embezzlement have all been used as tools of revenge by individuals who feel they've been wrongly blamed. Statistics are not available quantifying the annual cost of these types of responses to blame, but the numbers would astound if known.

Fortunately most organizations are not plagued with all of these side effects of blame at one time. Survival would certainly seem unlikely in that case. Yet, most organizations deal with all of these consequences at some point in time, and at some place within the organization.

Acme Plastics Revisited

In the Acme Plastics case study, the person most likely to be blamed is the plant manager. Let's call him Alex. He was responsible for the plant that produced the out-of-spec product. In addition, he wasn't even aware that the product shipped was out-of-spec. Given those two pieces of information, and nothing else, an average person might quickly conclude Alex was grossly negligent in performing his job – whether from incompetence or carelessness. The VP of marketing, who took the heat from Big Auto's purchasing manager, likely feels intensely victimized by Alex's screw up. So, we should not be surprised this VP would like to see Alex's head served up on a plate.

Now, if we put ourselves in the plant manager's perspective, the view looks different. If I'm Alex, here's what I see:

> *Three years ago I moved my young family to this small southern town and took over a new plant start-up. Since then, I've been working 60 hours a week and missing out on some premium time with my wife and kids. But I've managed to put the pieces together to get the plant up and running. And somehow we've kept up with the crazy growth demands from our contract with Big Auto. Every month they've added a new product to our production plan. This has required hiring and training new people, adjusting shift schedules, sourcing additional materials, and in some cases purchasing unfamiliar press equipment and incorporating it into our limited plant space.*
>
> *Every time marketing drops a new part design on us they think we should be jumping up and down for joy due to the added business. But, let me tell you, every one of my*

plant people is exhausted. They've been working demanding hours under enormous stress. Then, six months ago, one of the old presses we moved down here from corporate had a catastrophic breakdown that took two weeks to repair. For one day we missed Big Auto's order, but by the second day we had shifted production internally, and had arranged contract work on the outside to cover our orders. We were all proud of the response, but marketing was all ticked off because we put one of Big Auto's lines down for that day.

Once we got our machine back up and running, I asked all production teams to knock themselves out coming up with ways to speed up production, expand our total capacity, or reduce costs. They all responded like troopers. We had about a dozen different initiatives going on. However, one of the teams with a great idea missed catching a detailed specification in the customer's part order. So, their idea (which reduced product cost with no compromise of quality) ended up as an off-spec part. Big Auto's purchasing people, instead of looking into the viability of this part, just clobbered us for not following spec. I understand that the VP of marketing took some real heat on this deal. Now he's looking for blood from manufacturing and I think I'm the likely target.

How should Alex deal with this incoming bomb shell? He's in a tough spot. Most of the situational variables are stacked against him. *(1)* He comes from a different "tribe" than marketing. *(2)* The severity of outcome is high – Acme might lose the Big Auto account. *(3)* He has perceived knowledge and authority for the event. *(4)* The blamer has no familiarity with his circumstances. *(5)* He was present at "ground zero" the entire time the product was being produced. *(6)* He is already unpopular with marketing.

Alex's best hope for retaining his job (assuming he really wants to retain it) is a prompt and assertive response. Alex knows he shouldn't go it alone in talking to the VP of marketing, but his own boss – the manufacturing VP – is also on the blame list, and has agreed to let Alex tackle this one on his own. Acme's chief financial officer is a fan of Alex. He's seen what the plant's concerted efforts have done to Acme's bottom line, and he's willing to mediate the discussion between Alex and the marketing VP. Alex knows that he should have had better controls in place to prevent shipping an off spec product. But he also knows that, in reality, you spend your time setting up preventive measures for things you anticipate. And nobody at Acme (manufacturing, quality assurance, or marketing) saw this possibility or rang any warning bell.

Alex dusted off his copy of this book (he's already read it), turned to Chapter 8, and prepared his script for talking to the marketing VP (Vance):

> *Step 1: Vance, thanks for taking the time to meet with me on the Big Auto product spec issue. I want you to know I'm mortified that you had to take the full brunt of Big Auto's rage over our mistake in the plant. I know you work hard to maintain a strong relationship with them and this certainly doesn't help. (Be ready for Vance's emotional venting here.) I know you must feel like we've violated the Acme code of customer focus. (A bit more venting.)*

> *Step 2: You know, if Big Auto, or any of our customers, is unhappy, that's bad news for manufacturing as well as marketing. All of our management bonuses are based on profitability, so even though we come from different places, I do want to see successful long-term relationships as well. In fact, I took this job in hopes of advancing my career here at Acme, so when we have a problem with our product, I know it's a black mark on my reputation. And I know that no matter how much new business you bring in, we on our end have to deliver on those promises if we all want to be successful.*

> *Step 3: This latest problem occurred because I tried to get my production teams fired up about innovating for the customer's benefit. The team that changed the plastic mix*

thought they were helping cut costs. Where I screwed up was in not anticipating that a bunch of innovators turned loose could run us afoul of a customer requirement.

Step 4: What I'd like to do going forward is two things. First, I'd like to assist in resolving this problem with Big Auto. By my attending next week's meeting with their purchasing group, we can have them direct their anger at me as the cause of their problem, which leaves you free to redirect focus onto our proposed rebate solution. Also, sometimes when people are really angry, speaking directly to the culprit allows them to let go of their pent-up sense of hostility. Second, I'd like to get your Big Auto account manager involved in a meeting with quality assurance and my production leaders to develop a system to prevent unauthorized product changes in the future.

Step 5: What do you think on each of these ideas? (Work through any modifications and get commitment.)

Step 6: You know, Vance, I really appreciate your letting me come in here and try to get things back on track. I realize marketing and manufacturing often lock horns on issues. But I'm also smart enough to know that if Acme is going to be successful, then we need to continually find a way to work through problems. You've been at this a long time, is there anything you'd like to see from my end that would help keep us going forward productively?

If Alex works through this game plan, will he reduce enough of the blame directed at him to salvage his job? That's tough to say. It depends, in part, on how much of Vance's anger is due to the situation, and how much is due to his dislike of Alex. It depends on what happens with Big Auto. And, it also depends, in large part, to what extent Acme's president actively promotes a blame-free culture. But I do know that if Alex does nothing, his chances for a happy outcome are slim.

*****

And so it goes anytime you are caught in the cross-hairs of a blamer's sights. If your response is prompt, assertive, and smart (i.e. the six steps above) you might succeed in extricating yourself from blame. The cold reality, however, might be a blamer more obsessed with retribution for his pain, righteous administration of "justice," or possibly even the pleasure of seeing someone else squirm, than with problem resolution. As we discussed earlier in this book, there are many motivations for someone to cling to blame. Or, perhaps the blamer really does not like you, and hopes to inflict damage. Blame could just be the instrument of choice to engage in workplace bullying. In any of these cases, your battle is not over.

If you still wish to be cleared from the blame, you can explain to the accuser how continued adherence to blame, instead of focusing on process improvement, damages goal attainment for your organization. If the blamer becomes concerned that he will be viewed as obstructionist, he may relent. Next, you can insist on an impartial hearing by a board of arbitration. The simple threat of being found wrong may force the blamer to back down. If you're confident of your position, then the formal findings of an objective hearing might clear your way forward.

The other choice, of course, is to remove yourself from that environment. Is this a company you truly want to work for? Is this a relationship you truly want to maintain? Remember: your life will be better if you work with (and live with) people who understand the destructive nature of blame, who understand that in our systemic environment no cause exists in isolation, and who believe that people do things for reasons. Do you want to accept the pain of blame to continue your present circumstances? Or are you willing to face the unknown and begin a search for an environment less infected with blame? Only you can make that choice.

Endnotes

[1] Kurtzman, D. "Jokes About Hurricane Katrina," *About.com:Political Humor* http://politicalhumor.about.com/od/hurricanekatrina/a/katrinajokes_2.htm

[2] Kurtzman, D. "Jokes About Hurricane Katrina," *About.com:Political Humor* http://politicalhumor.about.com/od/hurricanekatrina/a/katrinajokes_2.htm

[3] "Punitive Damage Awards in Financial Injury Jury Verdicts," *Rand Institute for Civil Justice*, (1997). http://www.rand.org/pubs/research_briefs/RB9028/index1.html

[4] "Investigation of Defensive Medicine in Massachusetts," *Massachusetts Medical Society*, (November 2008). http://www.ncrponline.org/PDFs/Mass_Med_Soc.pdf

[5] Guadagnino, C. "Obstetrician Scarcity in Pennsylvania," *Physicians News Digest,* (May 23, 2004). http://www.physiciansnews.com/2004/05/23/obstetrician-scarcity-in-pennsylvania/

[6] "Emergency department directors see specialist shortages," *American Medical News*, (May 22/29, 2006). http://www.ama-assn.org/amednews/2006/05/22/prbf0522.htm

[7] Viscusi, W.K. "Liability," *Library of Economics and Liberty*. http://www.econlib.org/library/Enc/Liability.html

[8] Ibid.

[9] Cohen, J. "Is Liability Slowing AIDS Vaccines?" *Science*, (April 10, 1992).

[10] Mahoney, R. and Littlejohn, S. "Innovation On Trial: Punitive Damages Versus New Products," *Science*, (December 15, 1989).

[11] Stovsky, M. "Product Liability Barriers to the Commercialization of Biotechnology," *Berkeley Technology Law Journal*, (1992). http://www.law.berkeley.edu/journals/btlj/articles/vol6/Stovsky.pdf

[12] Douglas, T. *Scapegoat: Transferring Blame*, (London: Routledge, 1995).

[13] "The Malleus Maleficarum – Introduction to Online Edition," (2010). http://www.malleusmaleficarum.org/

[14] Kors, A.C. and Peters, E. eds. (2001) *Witchcraft in Europe 400-1700*. University of Pennsylvania Press.

[15] Brewer, E. "Dictionary of Phrase and Fable," *Bartleby Online*, (1898). http://www.bartleby.com/81/

[16] "Whipping Boy," *Wikipedia*, (2010). http://en.wikipedia.org/wiki/Whipping_boy

[17] "Proverbs Around the World," *MemorableQuotations.com*, (2010). http://www.memorablequotations.com/proverb.html

[18] "Karma," *New World Encyclopedia*, (2010). http://www.newworldencyclopedia.org/entry/Karma

[19] "Myanmar Conflict," *Centre for Humanitarian Dialogue*, (2010) http://www.hdcentre.org/newscred/topicpage/myanmar-conflict

[20] Miller, J.G. (1984) found that people from individualistic cultures are prone to fundamental attribution error while people from collectivistic cultures are less susceptible. Masuda, T. and Nisbett R.E. (2001) compared attention to social factors between American and Japanese cultures and suggested that Eastern cultures tend to attribute behavior to situation while Westerners attribute the same behavior to the individual.

[21] Taylor, S. *Cultureshock! France,* (Marshall Cavendish Corporation 3rd edition, 2008).

[22] Benoit-Nadeau, J. and Barlow, J. *Sixty Million Frenchmen Can't Be Wrong: Why We Love France But Not The French* (Sourcebooks, Inc. 2003).

[23] Jewish jokes are widely available on the internet. This one came from: http://www.jewishmag.com/50mag/humor/humor.htm

[24] I happened across this t-shirt for sale on the internet. I cannot attest to the validity of the site. And if you purchase one don't blame me if you end up paying in Purgatory for your heresy. http://www.zazzle.com/our_lady_of_perpetual_guilt_alumnus_tshirt-

235730127855081283

[25] Edward E Jones and Victor Harris (1967) hypothesized that people would attribute freely-chosen behaviors to disposition and chance-directed behaviors to situation. Later, Lee Ross (1977) coined the term fundamental attribution error.

[26] Miller, J.G. (1984) found that people from individualistic cultures are prone to fundamental attribution error while people from collectivistic cultures are less susceptible. Masuda, T. and Nisbett R.E. (2001) compared attention to social factors between American and Japanese cultures and suggested that Eastern cultures tend to attribute behavior to situation while Westerners attribute the same behavior to the individual.

[27] Bass, E. and Davis, L. *The Courage to Heal (A Guide for Women Survivors of Child Sexual Abuse.* (Collins Living, 1988).

[28] Staddon, J.E.R. and Niv, Yael, *Scholarpedia*, 3(9):2318, (2008). Skinner, B. F. *The behavior of organisms*, (New York: Appleton-Century-Crofts, 1938).

[29] Isom, M.D. "Albert Bandura – The Social Learning Theory," (1998). http://www.criminology.fsu.edu/crimtheory/bandura.htm

[30] Mearns, J. "The Social Learning Theory of Julian Rotter," (2004). http://psych.fullerton.edu/jmearns/rotter.htm

[31] http://www.psych.uncc.edu/pagoolka/LC.html
http://similarminds.com/locus.html
http://www.queendom.com/tests/access_page/index.htm?idRegTest=704

[32] Peterson, M. "Thomas Edison, Failure," *Invention & Technology Magazine*, Vol 6, Issue 3 (online), (1991). http://www.americanheritage.com/articles/magazine/it/1991/3/1991_3_8.shtml

[33] Taylor, S. "Optimism/Pessimism," *John D and Catherine T MacArthur Research Network on Socioeconomic Status and Health,* (1998). http://www.macses.ucsf.edu/research/psychosocial/optimism.php

[34] Seligman, M. "Interview: Martin Seligman on Optimism and Pessimism," (2007). http://www.learner.org/discoveringpsychology/12/e12expand.html

[35] Festinger, L. *A Theory of Cognitive Dissonance*, (Standford University Press, 1957).

[36] Kuhn, T. *The Structure of Scientific Revolutions*, (University Of Chicago

Press; 3rd edition, December 15, 1996).

[37] Barker, J. *Paradigms: The Business of Discovering the Future*, (HarperBusiness, 1993).

[38] Tavris, C. and Aronson, E. *Mistakes Were Made (but not by me)*, (Harcourt Books, 2007).

[39] Langer, G. "Rallying the Nation – Support for War Spikes as Bush Sets a Deadline," (2003). http://abcnews.go.com/sections/us/Living/iraq_war_poll030318.html

[40] Schneider, B. "Poll: Support for the Iraq War deteriorates," *CNN.com*, (2007). http://www.cnn.com/2007/POLITICS/03/19/iraq.support/index.html

[41] Nelesen, A. "Filling the Void Left Behind," *Green Bay Press Gazette*, (June 4, 2009).

[42] Auster, B. "One Amazing Kid," *U.S.News & World Report*, (1995). http://www.usnews.com/usnews/news/articles/950619/archive_010384.htm

[43] Andrews, E. "Greenspan Concedes Error on Regulation," *The New York Times*, (October 24, 2008). http://www.nytimes.com/2008/10/24/business/economy/24panel.html?ei=5124&en=00af9d0fc1ae268f&ex=1382500800&partner=digg&exprod=digg&pagewanted=print

[44] "25 People to Blame for the Financial Crisis," *Time Magazine*, (2008). http://www.time.com/time/specials/packages/completelist/0,29569,1877351,00.html

[45] "Rumsfeld Awaits Abu Ghraib Report," *BBC News (online)*, (August 24, 2004). http://news.bbc.co.uk/2/hi/americas/3593402.stm

[46] Belkin, L. "Parents Blaming Parents," *The New York Times Magazine*, (1999). http://www.nytimes.com/1999/10/31/magazine/parents-blaming-parents.html?n=Top/Reference/Times%20Topics/People/K/Klebold,%20Dylan&scp=4&sq=belkin%20klebold&st=cse&pagewanted=1

[47] "CBS News Poll: Columbine Shootings," (April 19, 2000). http://www.cbsnews.com/stories/2000/04/20/opinion/main186248.shtml

[48] "Americans Blame Parents, Not Guns." http://www.dadi.org/its_prnt.htm

[49] Goodwin, D. *Team of Rivals*. (Simon & Schuster, 2005).

[50] Aristotle, *Book Three: Nicomachean Ethics*, Translated by Martin Ostwald, (The Bobbs-Merrill Company, Inc. 1962).

[51] Ibid.

[52] Skyttner, L. *General Systems Theory: An Introduction*, (World Scientific Publishing Company, 1996).

[53] Kabat-Zinn, J. *Wherever You Go, There You Are*, (Hyperion, 1995).

[54] There are numerous variations of this poem, some believed to originate in the 14th century. However it is most frequently believed to be attributed to the death of Richard III of England in the Battle of Bosworth. In the 18th century Benjamin Franklin used variants of the poem in several writings.

[55] Von Bertalanffy, L. *General Systems Theory: Foundations, Development, Applications*, (New York: George Braziller, 1968).

[56] Ashby, R. *Introduction to Cybernetics*. (Routledge, Kegan, and Paul, 1956).

[57] Meadows, D. et al. *Limits to Growth*, (Universe Books, 1972).

[58] While Al Gore may have re-lit a candle under the climate change issue with his 2007 movie, *An Inconvenient Truth*, most of that information can be found in some form in the Club of Rome's report from over 30 years earlier.

[59] Forrester, J. *World Dynamics*, (Wright-Allen Press, 2nd edition, 1971).

[60] Wiley, J. "Blame air conditioning for Kerry loss," *The Casper Star-Tribune*, (December 5, 2004).

[61] "Butterfly Effect," *Wikipedia*, (2010). http://en.wikipedia.org/wiki/Butterfly_effect

[62] Whelan, E. "Ed Bradley's Mountain vs. John Stossel's Molehill," *American Council on Science and Health - Editorial*, (August 15, 2000). http://www.acsh.org/healthissues/newsID.249/healthissue_detail.asp

[63] Ladkin, P. & Stuphorn, J. Faculty of Technology, University of Bielefeld, Germany. "Two Causal Analyses of the Black Hawk Shootdown during Operation Provide Comfort," presented at the *8th Australian Workshop on Safety Critical Systems and Software*, (2003).

[64] "Tragedy over Iraq: Shootdown," *USA Today Information Network*, (April 15,

1994).

[65] Lowe, R. "Last Week's 'Friendly Fire' Tragedy Unlike Any Other," *Columbus Dispatch*, (April 19, 1994).

[66] "Pilots get blamed for copter downing," *Dayton Daily News*, (April 19, 1994).

[67] Lacayo, R., et al. "Deadly Mistaken Identity," *Time Magazine*, (April 25, 1994).

[68] "2 copters weren't "friendly," *Knight-Ridder Newspapers and Associated Press*, (April 19, 1994).

[69] Ladkin, P. & Stuphorn, J. Faculty of Technology, University of Bielefeld, Germany. "Two Causal Analyses of the Black Hawk Shootdown during Operation Provide Comfort," presented at the *8th Australian Workshop on Safety Critical Systems and Software*, (2003).

[70] Snook, S. *Friendly Fire*, (Princeton University Press, 2000).

[71] Deming, W.E. *Out of the Crisis*, (Massachusetts Institute of Technology, Center for Advanced Engineering Study, 1986). 275.

[72] Ibid. 248

[73] Ibid. 109

[74] Statistical Abstract of the United States, (2000).

[75] "Wacky Warning Labels," *The Michigan Lawsuit Abuse Watch*, (2010). http://www.mlaw.org/

[76] St.John, W. "Sorrow So Sweet: A Guilty Pleasure in Another's Woe," *New York Times*, (August 24, 2002).

[77] http://www.historyplace.com/speeches/churchill-hour.htm

[78] Interestingly, the impact of time works to the advantage of the accused in scandals involving politicians and other high-profile individuals. If the accused can maintain his/her position with no serious consequences long enough, the public eventually forgets the incident and moves on to other scandals.
[79] Gragg, C. "Whose Fault Was It?" *Harvard Business Review*, (January-February 1964).

[80] Deming, W.E. *Out of the Crisis,* (Massachusetts Institute of Technology, Center for Advanced Engineering Study, 1986).

[81] Gibbons, J. "I Can't Get No… Job Satisfaction, That Is," *The Conference Board*, (January 2010). http://www.conference-board.org/publications/describe.cfm?id=1727

[82] Arendt, L. "I Love My Job (not really)," *Corporate Report Wisconsin*, (February 2010).

[83] Vick, K. "Violence at work tied to loss of esteem," *St. Petersburg Times*, (December 17, 1993).

[84] Leingang, M. "Ohio State janitor's gunfire kills co-worker, self," *Yahoo News (Associated Press)* (March 9, 2010).

[85] "Workplace Violence," *Woods Hole Oceanographic Institution*, (2009). http://www.whoi.edu/services/HR/supervis/violence.html

www.ingramcontent.com/pod-product-compliance
Lightning Source LLC
Chambersburg PA
CBHW021418210526
45463CB00001B/436